CAROL PURVES

Chinese Whispers
The Gladys Aylward story

© Day One Publications 2004
First printed 2004

ISBN 1 903087 57-0

9 781903 087572

British Library Cataloguing in Publication Data available

Published by Day One Publications
Ryelands Road Leominster
Herefordshire HR6 8NZ ☎ 01568 613 740
email address: sales@dayone.co.uk
web site: www.dayone.co.uk

Designed by Steve Devane and printed by CPD

Contents

Set apart by God

The red of the rust blended with the red of the blood that was dripping down the handle of the axe, over the fist that held it, and down to mingle with the dirt on the ground.

Gladys stared into the demented eyes of the axeman. If ever she needed the protection of her God, it was now. Thoughts of Moses, Gideon, David, Samson all floated through her mind. God had saved them, the same God whom she worshipped. Her simple logic told her he would save her, but she was afraid.

'God help me, help me now.'

Her unspoken prayer shot up to heaven. She held out a shaky hand, her dark brown eyes still fixed firmly on the man.

'Give–it–to–me.'

In a quiet authoritative voice she spoke the words slowly and deliberately in her best Mandarin.

She waited. The prisoners huddled round the walls waited. The governor and officials outside the locked door waited. Even the birds seemed to hush their song and the wind paused on its journey across the mountains. Would the axeman obey the simple order, or would he add Gladys to his victims?

Our story begins far away from the bleak mountains of China, in the East End of London. It started at the end of the nineteenth century and the dawn of the twentieth. These were the last years of a way of life that would soon be gone for ever. Queen Victoria had just celebrated her Diamond Jubilee and the British Empire was at its peak; prosperity was great and Christian morals were held in high regard.

This may have been true for the upper classes, but for the poor it was a different story. Poverty was crippling and there was no help from the government. There was no child benefit, no sickness benefit, no old age pension. The dreaded workhouse became the final home for many.

It was in this environment that many philanthropists had discovered outlets for their compassion. Cadbury, Rowntree and Fry, were motivated by Christian love in their pioneering care for their employees, while Muller, Barnardo and Shaftesbury devoted themselves to caring for children.

The story of Gladys Aylward is also a story about caring for children, but not the children of London where she was brought up. God called Gladys to an unknown country, to speak a language very different from her mother tongue, and to love children and babies who looked very different from her former school friends.

Gladys' parents met through the Post Office where they both worked. Thomas Aylward was a postman and during the course of his work, he had to call into the office daily to collect the mail. He became attracted to the good-looking young girl behind the counter, Rosina Whiskin. She was a lively out-going Cockney, always laughing and joking, just the opposite of the shy, retiring Thomas.

Courting Rosina was going to be a problem to Thomas as he was too embarrassed to engage her in conversation. He resorted to slipping notes to her over the counter and eventually she agreed to a date. However, when it finally came round, he was so shy that he hid on the other side of the road.

'Thomas Aylward, why were you skulking on the other side of the road?'

The following morning, the slighted Rosina vented her full cockney vocabulary on the timid Thomas. In spite of such an unpromising start, their romance flourished and eventually, dressed in bright colours and feathers, which were so fashionable at the time, Rosina was married to Thomas on the 8 August 1900. They began their married life in Bermondsey but later moved to 6 Sunningdale Cottages, Bury Street, Edmonton.

Like many London suburbs in those days, Edmonton was a close-knit community. Family members found work nearby and rarely moved far from the vicinity. Problems and tragedies were shared, simple pleasures enjoyed and companionship found in either the churches or numerous public houses.

It was here on the 24 February 1902 that little Gladys May Aylward was born, an event celebrated only by close family and neighbours. Sunningdale Cottage soon proved too small for the young family so they moved to 67 Cheddington Street also in Edmonton. This was a terraced house with a small garden in an ordinary street and it was here that another daughter and a son were born to Rosina and Thomas.

Gladys, Violet and Laurence enjoyed an untroubled and care-free childhood. Edmonton at the beginning of the twentieth century, was surrounded by green fields and muddy potted roads. Birdsong could be heard above the sound of farm machinery and the clopping of horse's hooves. Long grass was for frolicking in, wild flowers for picking and fields for exploring. Rosina and Thomas didn't believe in shielding or over-protecting their children, but allowed them to lead their own lives.

Gladys liked to play, hop-scotch, hoops, or five stones. She found the games innocent and harmless and later described her family as a united one, 'finding our joy in the church and each other'.

The Aylwards were well connected with the church, as Thomas was the vicar's warden at St. Aldhelms Church, just round the corner. Rosina was an energetic woman, ahead of her time in many ways and having known the evils of drink in her own family, she became a speaker for the Temperance Movement. At many meetings Rosina spoke from the platform, while her three small children quietly played on the floor. Did young Gladys ever imagine she would one day be taking such meetings and drawing hundreds of hungry souls to hear her message?

Gladys attended Sunday School at the church, along with her brother and sister. She learned of missionaries who were taking the word of God to all corners of the world, but it had no personal meaning to her at that time.

Protected by the warmth of her family, Gladys was unaware of the Suffragette Movement that was prolific while she was a child. Neither was she aware of various improvements being made for those who were not financially well-off. Scouting for Boys was started in 1907 and the old-age pension was introduced the following year. In spite of these measures, by the time Gladys had started school there were serious strikes and much labour unrest.

'Gladys Aylward attacks her difficulties vigorously'

Her school reports gave a clue to the strength of character that was to reflect her whole life. The teachers could not comment on the excellence of her work and today she would probably have been diagnosed as dyslexic.

'As far as I remember, I never passed one exam at school', she said later.

The name of Gladys Aylward never featured on an examination result board at Silver Street School, which was less than a quarter of a mile from her home. However, in later years it was renamed 'The Aylward School' in her honour.

Nevertheless, she was earnest about her work, in spite of finding it difficult to grasp. Arithmetic especially remained an enigma; however, her teachers would comment on her conduct and personal neatness.

Only five feet in stature, she was short even for her generation. Her height, or lack of it, along with the determination in her eyes, were the features most remembered by people who met her during her life. Gladys was never very strong, she often suffered ill-health and missed some of her schooling, which did little to help her education.

Gladys in London, 1928

In 1916, aged fourteen, she left school without any qualifications at a time when work was hard to find. Her first job was at Marks and Spencers, which was then a 'Penny Bazaar'. Later she worked in a grocer's shop. She was well suited to the retail trade with her pleasant manner and ease with people. However, when the men came back from the war in 1918 she had to leave these jobs and go into service.

The employment situation was very fragile. There were two million unemployed by 1921 and in 1926 came the General Strike.

With her restless spirit, Gladys never stayed anywhere for long, but eventually trained as a parlour maid and went into gentleman's service. Although not clever, she was quick and looked very smart in her black dress and pretty apron with a bow in her hair. She became conversant with many notable people of that time which was later to stand her in good stead in her work in China.

Going into service meant leaving home, and moving to the West End of London where life was very different from Edmonton. Gladys noticed the way the rich dressed and lived; the ladies in furs and jewels; the gentlemen in long tails and top hats. Yet side by side with wealth was poverty. Hidden down the side streets, Gladys witnessed first hand the ragged children, tramps sleeping rough, and scarlet lipped and heavily powdered faces of street women. Other sights were more welcome; the London buses, the letter boxes painted bright red, the police and newsvendors. The London parks were full of mothers or maids pushing prams with babies heavily wrapped up against the variable weather.

The city lights, the music halls, the restaurants and the theatres were all new to her. London life was full of temptation, but she had little time or money to indulge. Her favourite leisure activity was to visit was the theatre with Queenie, her cousin, where the first sound films appeared in 1927. Gladys even dreamed of going on the stage herself or being a film star in Hollywood. This was not such an idle dream. She had the power of mimicry and story telling, inherited from her mother, and charisma, which could hold audiences captive.

Gladys started going to drama classes on her free evenings. She learned many things that had been instinctive to her before. She learned to throw her voice and the power of the dramatic pause. How she loved that pause and pictured her audience waiting spell-bound for what she would say next. It was a strategy she was to employ with great effect all her life.

Gladys was not altogether happy with her looks. To be a film star she knew she should be better looking. At only five foot tall, she was too short. She would also have loved long, blonde, wavy hair instead of her straight dark locks. Back in the 1920s she didn't know that one day she would give thanks to God for her looks.

Life for Gladys might have continued in this way, for many years, except for an event one Tuesday evening in 1925. Away from the religious restraints of her home and godly influence of her parents, Gladys had developed a taste for the pleasures of the world. She was on the way to a dance with some of her friends when her party got muddled up in the crowded street with a group of young people going into a service in Aubrey Church (later Kensington Temple) in Kensington Park Road.

Gladys found herself separated from her friends and however hard she pushed her small frame, she could not get through. Almost lifted off her feet, she was hustled into the church and as the service had started she felt too shy to get up and leave. She shuffled uncomfortably in her seat thinking back to the days she attended church before leaving home. Suddenly, she felt the speaker was talking directly to her. She had heard similar messages in the past, but they had not seemed so personal to her. God was claiming her attention.

On this particular evening, she heard a young man talking about mission. Glady knew there were missionaries but felt they were of no particular interest to her, except to give them a few coins in the collecting plate. However, on this evening her soul was stirred. She later wished she could have told the young man how much she was moved.

As she left the meeting in a trance, the vicar's wife, who knew who she was, said to her, 'Miss Aylward, I believe God is wanting you'.

The Holy Spirit was working in her life and these words became a personal challenge to Gladys. As she reflected on this conviction in the coming weeks, she realised that God wanted her to give her life to him, that he had work for her to do.

It was the beginning of the greatest adventure of her life.

Tenfold blessings

Gladys had no doubt that God wanted her to spend her life in his service. She felt a calm and peacefulness she had never known before; she had found her purpose in life—serving God.

Her personality did not radically change overnight, but she found that things which had been important to her became less important. The love of the cinema and acting remained with her, but they became secondary interests. Her talent never left her, but now it was consecrated to God and he would in due course make full use of it. The acting lessons were not wasted; Gladys had learned to stir great crowds emotionally and God was going to use that in the future!

Her job as a parlour maid ceased to be an end in itself. It became the source of income, which she used for God to help prepare her for the next step. Her ability to mix with her own class and those of the upper classes was useful training for her future life.

It appeared to Gladys that everything that had happened so far had just been a preparation for what was to come.

Her family were a close knit group who prayed and encouraged her, and who stood by her when she felt all others, except God, had deserted her. It was to her sister Vi that Gladys was to write during the lonely China years.

Although Gladys knew that God wanted her whole life, she did not yet know how. Opportunities in Christian service for a young girl in the 1920s were limited. What did God want Gladys Aylward to do? Was she being called to service in England or abroad? If she was to be a missionary, where should she go? She prayed and waited. She was not idle and she started going to the Young Life Campaign meetings.

Having always been close to her cousin Queenie, she took her along. Because of Gladys' enthusiasm, Queenie thought these meetings were like tea-parties for old ladies with Gladys in charge.

Gladys felt strengthened and uplifted by their hymn singing. Her ability to play the piano proved useful in the Bible Classes and extempore prayer came easily to her. From this time onwards she regarded God as her best friend and her prayers reflected that. The testimonies she heard thrilled her;

and made her wish that like others, she had a great story to tell. She felt her life and experiences had been ordinary so far, but what she did not fully realise was that God was working in her life.

One day sitting on the top deck of a bus, Gladys was reading the *Young Life Campaign* magazine.

Planes can now fly over the vast country of China, but there are millions there who have never heard the gospel.

Gladys jerked upright in her seat and gasped. She knew air travel was still in its infancy, but this article told of a plane that had flown up the route of the Yellow River from Shanghai to Lanchow. Amazing though this was, what really grabbed Gladys' attention was the thousands who had never heard the Good News.

She did some research. China was a country only slightly smaller than USA consisting of some three and three quarter thousand square miles. A quick look at a map showed her this vast country, the world's fourth largest, had borders with Russia, Korea, Mongolia, Nepal, Pakistan and even Afghanistan.

There were 9,000 miles of coastline and a diverse climate ranging from tropical in the south to sub-arctic in the north. The country was mostly mountainous with high plateau and deserts in the west with plains, deltas and hills in the east. The coastal regions suffered frequent typhoons while other areas saw damaging floods, earthquakes and droughts from time to time.

Gladys could not really grasp the vastness of this huge land. England seemed so small in comparison. She was also appalled that such a large country had so small a Chrisitian witness. In Britain, there were churches up and down the country, Christian literature was everywhere and many people were Christians. How keenly Gladys felt for the Chinese who were living and dying without having heard of Christ. She resolved that something must be done.

Gladys started a one-woman campaign. She would persuade someone to go to China as a missionary. She started by contacting all the important people she knew. Only the best was good enough for God. Some talented and clever person must go there.

She approached doctors, clergymen, bank mangers, and solicitors. She wrote to the wealthy and influential people whom she knew slightly or whom she had met in the course of her work. Most of them were surprised to be approached by this pint-sized, enthusiastic woman, but without exception they all declined. In some cases the refusal was not even polite!

Gladys was in despair. She knew someone had to go to China. Suddenly she thought of her brother, Laurence. A drummer in the army, he was strong, upright and presentable and also the right age. She resolved to challenge him at the next opportunity.

She did not have long to wait. One afternoon they were sitting together in the living-room of their parent's house. Gladys knew this might be her only chance, so she sat tensely on the edge of her chair. In prayer, she had told God that if her brother would not go to China, he would be the last person she would ask. After this she would give up thinking about it.

Laurence stood to leave the room. Gladys knew she had to speak out: 'Laurence, there are thousands in China who have never heard about God. Will you go and tell them?'

Laurence looked at his older sister in amazement. He knew she had many strange ideas, but this was the most bizarre. He had his career, and his comfortable life-style. He was not particularly concerned about heathen foreigners half way round the world! He reached the door and was nearly out the room. With his hand on the door, he looked back at Gladys, a boyish grin on his face: 'Me go to China as a missionary! That's a job for an old maid. If you're so keen why don't *you* go yourself.'

Gladys sat stock-still. Me go to China! A dozen excuses flew into her mind. God would never want her to go abroad. She was young, female and her health was not strong. She wasn't clever, never having passed an exam at school. God should have the very best and she certainly considered she was not the best.

These thoughts went round and round in her mind. For days she could think about nothing else. She argued with herself this way and that, but God continued to convict her because it was Gladys he wanted in China. One evening she bowed her head in prayer before God. She would go to China.

When Gladys told her father, he was very sceptical of her abilities.

'What are you going to do out there? Can you nurse?'

'No.'

'Can you teach?'

'No.'

'All you can do is talk.'

And that is what Gladys decided she could do. If God wanted her to talk, she would. She would talk her way into the hearts of the Chinese. To give herself practice she started speaking at Hyde Park Corner. What a picture she cut! A small diminutive figure, proclaiming the good news of Christ, among the great orators of the day. Not many people listened, but Gladys knew the experience was invaluable.

She started sending small sums of money to the China Inland Mission for the despatch of Bibles to China. With the acknowledgement of the gifts came literature describing the work of the Mission. It was the CIM that Gladys considered when she began to think about the training she would need.

On a crisp Wednesday morning in January 1930, Gladys went for the interview at the Bible College. She was not sure what to expect, but had dressed up in her most presentable clothes, leaving off any jewellery as she did not want to give the wrong impression.

The interview with the Principal of the college did not go well.

'Why do you want to go to China?'

'I believe God wants me to work for him there.'

'Good, but what qualifications do you have. What exams have you passed?'

'None.'

'I see. Well, how well read are you? What do you feel about the life of Hudson Taylor?'

'Who was he?'

It was a wonder the interview went any further after that. To not know about the founder of the CIM at a CIM interview was quite typical of Gladys. It was her nature to jump in first and think afterwards. When questioned, neither did she know how missionary work had been started in China in the middle of the nineteenth century by Elijah Coleman Bridgman.

'You have no qualifications. You haven't passed any exams. You would still need to learn Chinese. All I can do is to give you one term's trial.'

In the Mission's records, the Principal stated that at the age of eighteen, Gladys had been brought face to face with her own need and was converted. She had been a constant source of witness wherever she worked and at open-air meetings and childrens' services. Even at the interview, he recognised and acknowledged her great strength of character, but was worried by her lack of education.

Early in 1930, Gladys started at Aberdeen Park, Highbury, at the Woman's Training Home for the CIM. She was now living and working with a group of women, all training to go out to China and there were many different experiences for her. She fitted in well though and enjoyed the prayer meetings, the discipline, the domestic chores and the personal evangelism they had to do.

What she did not enjoy was the lectures and study. She tried her best, but she could not make sense of much of it. Her enthusiasm just could not make up for her lack of ability to remember what she was learning. She tried to make some sense of the Chinese language , but it was quite beyond her. Without using the twenty-six letters of our alphabet she was absolutely lost.

'It just won't go in', Gladys said to her fellow students. They were struggling, but making progress, but Gladys found she was not grasping it at all. Surely if God wanted her in China he would help her.

In April, the Principal sent for her again. He had received reports on her progress. It stated she had engaged in the ordinary studies and practical work, but simple tests had revealed her limitations.

As Gladys stood in front of the large imposing desk she could see he was looking uncomfortable.

'Miss Aylward,' he began diffidently, 'I'm so sorry, but you just have not been able to cope with your studies this term. You haven't been able to learn all you have needed to learn. Maybe in your late twenties, you're too old to grasp the Chinese language. You started to learn too late. I can't allow you to waste any more of your time or ours. You will have to leave.'

He tried to soften the blow.

'If you have nothing planned for the future, I know of two retired missionaries in Bristol. They would be pleased to have you help them. They were in China for many years and through them and their connections, you will still be doing work linked to the Chinese.'

Gladys stood outside the Principal's door and silently wept. She was so sure God had wanted her in China. Had she made a mistake? Did God just intend her to work among the Chinese in this country? She knew she must be brave and try to make a success of her new life in Bristol.

Moving to the West Country, Gladys found Dr and Mrs Fisher very kind, but she was a sad and disappointed young lady when she worked for them. Feigning an enthusiasm she did not feel, she threw herself into her work. Inside she was confused and questioned God, feeling sure he wanted her in China, not the West of England.

She later moved to Neath, but didn't feel there was sufficient work for her there so she then moved to the dock area of Swansea to work with a couple she had known in London. Known as Sister Rescue, she spent her time in a hostel for working women. She did not really know what she wanted to do. All her waking thoughts had been of China but it seemed impossible that she could ever go there and her frustration continued. Gladys did not realise her experience with the needy in Swansea would be a preparation for China. She didn't realise that God was working in his time not hers.

She took a job as an assistant matron at the Sunshine Hostel and what she witnessed there was a preparation for later life. Her plan was to be generous to those that were needy in the hope that they would come to the mission meetings. Her plan worked in part but there were disappointments.

The work in South Wales had to stop when her mother became ill. As the eldest daughter, she felt she should return to London to be with her. She also felt she could earn more money if she went back to being a parlour maid.

A new job gave her new challenges, but only three days after starting, her mind was in a whirl. God was challenging her and calling her.

Eventually she could stand it no longer. In the quietness of her own room she placed her Daily Light and Bible on the bedside table. On top of these she placed all the money she possessed, 2½p. Falling on her knees, she prayed as she had never prayed before:

'O God, here is my Bible, here is my money, here am I. Please use us, God, please use us.'

Rising from her feet, she made two resolutions, which she tried to keep all her life. Firstly, never again would she ask someone else to do a job God was asking her to do. Secondly, if God would show her the way, she would go to China even if it means being unsponsored.

She had hardly finished praying before there was a knock on the door. It transpired that the mistress of the house wanted to see her. Puzzled, Gladys went down to the drawing room.

'Miss Aylward', the lady said, 'as you are new to this house, I need to explain. Whenever I have new staff, I always give them the fare they paid to get here. How much was yours?'

'Two shilling and ninepence from Edmonton, Madam.'

'Then here is three shillings.'

Gladys rushed upstairs to her room. God had answered her prayer quicker than she could have imagined. She was able to add three shillings to her savings, which had now increased more than ten-fold. Her mind started to work rapidly. To get to China she would need to pay her own fare. This money was the first instalment.

She was proving the truth of the text she so loved:

'My God shall supply all your needs.'

Preparations for China

Gladys thought of nothing now, except preparing for China. Her father had told her all she could do was talk, but she knew she needed more practice in front of crowds, so off she went to Hyde Park Corner again. A small person in drab clothes, she was hardly noticed among the more colourful figures, but the opposition she encountered, was going to stand her in good stead for the future. The persecution in China was going to be far worse than anything she received on the streets of London.

Earning money to pay for her fare to China also became a top priority. If a missionary society would not support her to go there, she would go without their help. Her small amount of savings was slowly increasing

On her next day off, she went to Mullers, a Travel Agents in London's Haymarket, where she had a bizarre conversation.

'How much is the fare to China?' she asked the bemused man behind the counter.

China was over five thousand miles away and very few people needed information about it. The clerk's face took on a grave expression and Gladys could only imagine the thoughts that were going through his head. He'd had many strange requests before, but this would be one of the strangest. She knew he was looking at a slight young lady, whose dress and demeanour indicated that she was in service. Would he think she was asking on behalf of her master or mistress?

'£90 by sea and £47 overland on the Trans-Siberian Railway.' he said curtly.

'Then I'll have to go over land, but I can't pay for it all at once.' Gladys explained. 'I'll pay in instalments. Here's the first instalment of £3.'

'But you don't understand. You can't travel by train. There's a civil war raging.'

'Oh, that doesn't matter. By the time I've paid the complete fare, the war will be over.'

The clerk then uttered words that Gladys was to remember many months later: 'We do like to deliver our customers alive and not dead.'

Gladys got her way. As she received her wages each week, she rushed to Mullers and paid another instalment towards her ticket.

Her next employment was with Sir Francis Younghusband who had been a soldier, author and explorer in China. Gladys desperately wanted to know more about the country to which God had called her so she devised a plan. After she finished her job dusting the well-stocked library, she would smuggle one of the books on China up to her room. She reckoned no-one would miss them.

Each night she read far into the early hours, eagerly devouring the information they contained. But her secret didn't remain undetected long. One morning she was summoned into the presence of the eminent man himself.

Standing just inside the large oak doors, she faced the angry bearded explorer.

'Miss Aylward, have you been stealing books from my library?'

Gladys was dismayed.

'Oh, no sir,' she stammered. 'I was only borrowing them.'

'Borrowing them? What for?'

'You see, sir, I want to be a missionary in China and I want to learn all I can about the country before I go.'

'A missionary. But you're a parlour maid.'

'I know, sir. But I believe God wants me in China.'

Sir Francis was sceptical, but kind.

'Well I suppose there's no harm in you borrowing books, but one at a time, mind. And make sure you take great care of them. There're very expensive.'

The fulfilment of God's plan was slowly taking place.

The next piece of the jigsaw happened during a missionary meeting where she was helping her mother. The speaker, who had spent some time in China, was talking about a Scottish missionary, a Mrs Jeannie Lawson.

Mrs Lawson had just returned to China after to period in England. She had travelled out to work in the Shensi district. From her studies of China, Gladys now knew exactly where that was. It was a remote area far up in the mountains. Few westerners had ever travelled there, the only visitors being the mule trains, which travelled along the rugged tracks from city to city.

Jeannie had served in other parts of China for many years as a missionary with her husband. When he died she returned to England, but her love for China and the lost Chinese souls was so great that at the age of seventy-three she had returned. She knew she wanted to die in China, but before she returned there, she had sent out a request for a person to carry on the work when she died. She needed a younger person to help her.

During that afternoon the plea was relayed to the congregation. Was there anyone present who felt the call to China? Gladys could hardly contain herself. She felt her soul cry out: 'That's me, Lord, that's me.'

Jeannie Lawson had now returned to China, but Gladys wrote to her. She was so excited when she received the reply. Yes, Jeannie would love to receive her out in China. All Gladys had to do was to pay for her own fare and Jeannie would arrange to meet her. It was imperative now for Gladys to finish paying for this ticket as soon as possible.

It was no easy task. She did everything she could. She took on extra work during her days off and cut down on fares and food whenever she could. Most young girls of her age collected for a bottom drawer, items that could be used when they got married and set up their own home. Gladys sold the few items she had accumulated. The call to China was greater.

She did anything that would give her money. She worked day and night, washed up in hotels, served at dinner parties, scrubbed floors and even worked as a kitchen maid.

Some of her measures were more extreme. Woolworth's in Oxford Street had a large bin of items all for three or six pence. Rummaging through the items, Gladys found two left shoes of her size. After she had bought them and put them on, she went to the Portabello Road and sold her own expensive leather ones, saying .It's all for China'.

She told nobody until later that she travelled all the way to China in shoes that were both for left feet. She never regretted the purchase of the shoes, but her feet later paid the price.

One day her mistress asked Gladys to accompany her to a garden party. She noticed Gladys had no suitable clothes, so she allowed her to choose something from her own wardrobe. After the party, the mistress commented that she looked so nice in the clothes she could keep them. Gladys was able to wear them until she left for China. The money she saved from buying any other clothes was 'All for China'.

Eventually, the great day arrived. As Gladys walked along the London streets her feet hardly touched the ground, in spite of her shoes, for in her pocket was her train ticket to Vladivostok. She kept feeling it to make sure it was still there. God had been faithful. Instead of taking three years to save enough money, it had only taken her until the autumn. She now had the means to get to China plus a welcome from Jeannie Lawson when she arrived. No time could be lost.

Gladys suffered from mixed emotions. She was so happy to be going, but how could she bear to leave her family and friends? She tried to grasp what a great sacrifice it was for her parents. They were allowing their eldest daughter to go half way round the world to an unknown country and situation. It was very likely that they would never see her again. Gladys knew it was only in the strength of God they were able to do it with a willing spirit.

A valedictory service was held for Gladys on the 29 September 1932. Many tears were shed. Her church members promised to pray for her regularly. They were mostly people with limited funds, but they gave what they could to this brave little woman. A single lady, a music teacher, from the church where Rosina attended, was able to give her a small folding stool. It meant there was more for Gladys to carry, but the stool was to prove immeasurably useful during the frozen Siberian winter. This lady also supported Gladys financially for the next seventeen years.

Gladys had no spare money to pay for items she needed to take with her. She had one small suitcase, in which she planned to keep her clothes. She had been able to buy a spirit stove for one and threepence and someone had kindly given her a kettle and saucepan. These items meant she would be able to cook food for herself as she travelled.

The journey would be through the Siberian winter, so she took a bedding roll made out of Rosina's woollen living room curtain, which she intended to tie on to her case with a piece of string. She had been given an old fur coat, which could double up for use as a rug.

In her corset Gladys was to carry her passport, tickets, fountain pen, two travellers cheques for £1 each and a small Bible. All these items were too precious to lose.

There still remained the problem of how she was to carry all her food.

She would be completely unable to buy any on the journey. For one thing there was no money left for provisions and for another she wouldn't know how or where to buy it. Three thousand miles was a very long journey, but once again, God provided. On the night before her departure a friend, later known to be Ivy, anonymously left another small suitcase outside the family home. Like all the gifts this was a sacrifice. Into this case Gladys was able to put her English food hoping it would be enough to sustain her over the miles.

The greatest sacrifice was emotional. Gladys loved her parents, her sister Vi and Lawrence. The journey to China was so long and she didn't know when, if ever, she would see them again.

More difficult was the suffering she was causing them. In her obedience to God; 'Blessed are those who forsake father and mother for my sake', she was the source of unhappiness to them. Gladys knew they were pleased for her and proud of her, but she guessed Rosina and Thomas would have been happier if her calling had been to London. Their beloved 'Glad' was stepping out into the unknown.

The morning of 15 October 1932 was cold and damp. It was decided the family would see her off on the train at Liverpool Street Station. At the last moment Thomas decided he couldn't face the parting and went to work instead. As Gladys travelled up to London with the others, she imagined her father having a quiet cry in some private place and Gladys sighed.

Standing bravely on the station platform, Gladys looked as if she was never even going to get out of England, let alone travel across two continents. In her hands she carried the two small suitcases, one filled with food, one with clothes. The home-made bedding roll was tied on with string. Her food case contained tins of sardines, corned beef, hard boiled eggs, Oxo cubes, crispbreads and plain soda cakes.

The steam from the waiting train mingled with the London fog. All was hustle and bustle on the station and there was no time to day-dream. Other groups were having tearful partings, though few could have been travelling so far. Porters rushed to and fro loading suitcases into the luggage van. Gladys' family busied themselves with the trivia of getting her safely on board.

Their small party on the platform made a pathetic picture. A few people from church and close neighbours had arrived to wish their own Gladys 'God speed'. It wasn't every day that one of their number journeyed to China, yet they hung back from her immediate family. They knew how poignant this parting was.

Gladys got on the train, found her seat and placed her few belongings next to it. Never had an expedition half way round the world been so poorly equipped, but never had one been undertaken with so much love. Gladys alighted for the last embrace, the last stammered words of parting.

Rosina and Vi stood close together with their winter coats wrapped tightly round them. The handkerchiefs they were using on their eyes, would all too soon be used to wave at the disappearing train.

The piecing shriek of the guard's whistle cut through the sounds of the noisy station. After the briefest and tightest of hugs Gladys scrambled back on to the train. The snorting of the engine silenced any further speech. Slowly the train inched forward and Gladys leaned out of the window as far as she dared. Rosina and Vi waved their crumpled white handkerchiefs as hard as they could. Gladys watched as her family and friends became tiny specks on the disappearing platform. She thought of Abraham.

Europe and Asia

As the train travelled through the Essex countryside, Gladys tried to imprint the scenes on her mind. In China there would be no rolling hills, nor farm buildings surrounded by patchwork fields. She was not sure whether the trees and plants would be different or the same. The few books she had been able to read hadn't explained details like that.

She wasn't too sure what the conditions would be like in China at all. She just knew she was obeying God's instructions; she would find out the details later. All she had to do now was to trust.

She sat sadly in her seat. The various emotions going through her mind had left her exhausted. Grouped round her tiny body were her few belongings. Was she mad to be embarking on such a journey? Ahead of her could be insurmountable difficulties but then she felt the shape of her Bible nestling in her corsets. She remembered the God who was sending her into the unknown was the same God who had cared for Abraham and would surely care for her. Nothing was too difficult for him. She recalled the words that were becoming so important to her, 'My God shall supply all your needs.'

At Harwich, Gladys changed on to the ferry to Flushing. She squeezed into a quiet corner seat, a small lonely figure, her large brown eyes observing the surroundings with wonder. Sailing was a new experience to Gladys and she was not too sure if she was enjoying it, but fortunately the crossing was smooth.

Arriving at Flushing, she then had to board a train to take her across Holland. She had hardly spoken to anyone since leaving her family and friends at Liverpool Street Station and was feeling lonely already.

Finding another corner seat, she settled down for further silent travelling. She hardly noticed the couple sitting opposite, but they had noticed her.

'Were you the little lady we saw on Liverpool Street Station, waving goodbye to all your friends?' the woman asked.

'Yes, that was me.' Gladys had been too wrapped up in her farewells to notice anyone else.

'Where are you going to?'

'China.'

'China! That's a long way. Why are you going there?'

'I'm going to be a missionary.'

The couple exchanged glances and then the man spoke.

'We've just been to a Christian convention at Keswick, but we haven't had the chance to meet a real live missionary.'

After this, the journey seemed to fly by. They had so much to say to each other. Gladys couldn't believe that only a little time before she had been feeling lonely. God must have known her feelings. The husband worked in the Dutch parliament and had a great deal to tell Gladys about that country.

When they got off the train, the wife said to Gladys, 'I promise that every day for the rest of my life we will pray for you at 9pm'

As they left the train and shook hands with Gladys, they left something in her hand. When she looked down, she realised they had given her a Scofield testament and a £1 note. Gladys thought she would never be able to spend English currency in China, but the time was going to come when that pound note would help to save her life.

Alone again as the train travelled across Germany, Gladys had difficulty in making herself understood by the ticket collectors. Her attempts at conversation were noticed by a German girl sitting further down the compartment. Her English was good enough for Gladys to understand. They sat talking, as best they could, until the train reached Berlin. Then her new German friend gave Gladys an invitation of which she was most grateful. Would Gladys like to spend the night in her flat? She most certainly would and during the evening, she was shown round Berlin. It felt different from anywhere in England, but she found it very interesting. After this break, Gladys resumed her journey across Germany, Poland, into Russia and on Tuesday 18 October, she recorded in her diary that they had arrived at one of the main stations in Moscow. What she saw there gave her a shock.

The people on the station seemed to have all their possessions with them. They just seemed to sit around and did not appear to be going anywhere. Could they be living in the station?, Gladys wondered.

'The lot of children seems very hard', she noted in her diary.

Subconsciously she was noting the plight of children even then. Her heart was being made ready for her future work. The children she saw were working or staggering along under great burdens. Children as young as five could be seen labouring on the roads.

She also noticed the women. They seemed to be doing all the heavy work, including carrying luggage. It was women who kept the stations clean, which were bare, except for essentials.

Gladys found that the toilets on the train were clean and she was able to wash and brush up every day. At night she was able to curl her hair, put on a smart cap and say her prayers before going to sleep. She ignored any strange looks she received, or was oblivious to them.

At the main station of Moscow she saw many soldiers who all looked dirty and untidy. They carried bread under their arms and just broke off a lump and ate it as they walked along. She also noted they spat and blew their noses on the ground. She shuddered, appalled by what she saw. This nation's culture was so far removed from her own country.

In her diary Gladys began by faithfully recording what she ate each day. 'For my meal I had Ryvita, a boiled egg and a cup of tea; at 11 o clock I had an Oxo drink.' She was most appreciative of her stove, saucepan and kettle. No food was available for travellers and in any case, Gladys couldn't afford to buy any.

Although she was distressed by what she saw in Russia, she guessed she was to see far worse sights in her missionary work.

On Wednesday 19 October, the train stopped for water about 7.30am. A nice young man went and filled her kettle. He had been one of her three companions during the night. In spite of being completely alone in a foreign land, Gladys experienced no fear. She had put her whole faith in God.

There was a routine to the train travel, which Gladys soon got used to. Each morning the feather mattresses were folded away to leave space in the compartments, while floating feathers still remained in the carriages for a while. The passengers then filed down to the toilet compartment. After that, the travellers had their breakfasts and Gladys ate her usual egg and Ryvita. The salt and pepper pots, which she used, were a source of great amusement to her companions. She shook some of the condiments onto their food, which they ate with great relish.

By Friday 21 October she was feeling a little miserable. She had been four whole days without hearing an English voice. Communication with others was difficult, but she did not stay sad for long. Her daily readings sustained her and in spite of her water supply decreasing she was able to praise God that she didn't need much to drink.

The track at this stage was very rough. Because of the lack of any chance for exercise, Gladys had a very small appetite, in spite of the good food she still had left. Coffee, Ryvita, dates and baked beans kept her going through these difficult days.

Saturday 22 October 1932 was the day they crossed the border into Siberia and had to change trains. The sight of the Siberian countryside was another cause for praise as the landscape was now snow-covered. In her innocence she found it hard to comprehend how the bright sun did not melt the thick snow. It was cold, too. A tin of herring roes, which she had only half eaten the day before, became frozen in the cup.

On Monday 24 October, a man entered the train who could speak English. His command of the language was very poor, but at least it was better than none. She then had an exhausting time answering all his questions and those that other travellers put to him. She was also able to ask him some questions.

He told her that trains were not running to Harbin and this one would probably be held up on the Siberian-Manchurian border. This meant it would be difficult for her to travel beyond Harbin to Dairen where she was to catch a steamer to Tientsin. Her head was bursting by the time he got out.

She was so worried by the news that she went to bed without supper that night and hardly knew what to do. To give herself courage, she got out her Bible to read one of her favourite parts where God brought the children of Israel out of bondage. A piece of paper fell out which she had been given in Bristol.

'Be not afraid—remember the Lord' (Nehemiah 4: 14)

She was so overcome, that she wept. Here she was worrying about her journey, while God had been helping her all the way. She realised how weak she was, and that her courage was only borrowed from him, but he would never let her down. She knew she would not turn back, even if she could.

She believed God would continue to reveal himself in a wonderful way.

At this part of the journey, many soldiers got on the train at each station, but Gladys still was not afraid. Two of the officers were with her during the night and she found it frustrating that they could not converse together. In the morning they all got off and stiffly marched away like the toy soldiers she had manoeuvred with Vi and Lawrence so long ago on the living room floor back in Edmonton. Eyeing her bedding roll, she remembered.

Gladys was now completely alone on the train. The conductor tried to persuade her to get off, but she was determined to stay as long as she could. She felt that each mile in the train was one mile nearer China.

A few hours later the train stopped again and all the lights went out. In the distance above the howling wind, she could hear a sound she had never heard before—gunfire. She suddenly remembered the chilling words of the clerk at Mullers in London: 'We do like to deliver our customers alive, and not dead.'

It was not until later that Gladys heard of the unofficial war between Russia and China for control of the Chinese Eastern Railway. Trains would stay where they were for days or months and then return with the casualties from the war. Reluctantly, Gladys got off the train and approached four men on the platform; the guard, driver, fireman and conductor. From their hand signals, her worst fear was confirmed. The train would go no further.

Ahead was the battlefield. Behind, far behind was the station where Gladys might be able to get another train. Between were miles of snow-covered track deep in Siberian forest. Gladys had no choice but to walk back along the track to civilisation.

With a heavy heart she picked up her few possessions and stepped out again into the unknown. Her two left shoes were very uncomfortable and her luggage bulky. Night was falling and she needed all her faith in God to keep going.

The silence was deafening, only broken by a slither of snow falling off tall pine trees, or the distant howling of dogs. At least that is what Gladys in her innocence thought they were!

'I wonder who let those dogs out on a night like this?' she said to herself.

In fact they were a pack of hunting wolves and very dangerous for humans. The night was wild and cold, as only a Siberian night in October can be and the biting wind was cutting through Gladys' fur coat. After a few hours she could go no further.

Gathering her few belongings round her, she lit her stove to boil her kettle. She placed her cases round as a wind break, and pulled the fur coat tighter on her frozen shoulders. As she drifted off into a fitful sleep, Gladys was not sure if she would survive the freezing night. She did not know if she would ever be any nearer to China than she was now.

Was this to be her last night on earth? Would she die beside the Trans Siberian Railway, alone and unknown?

Even further east

Consciousness was returning; Gladys gently flexed her fingers. She was relieved she could still move them. She wriggled her arms and shoulders. It was very early in the morning, but Gladys was too cold to sleep any more. The pale sun was shining through the trees. She had actually slept very little as it had been far too cold. With a shudder she sat up; she hadn't died—God had kept her safe. He still had work for her to do.

She had a long way to go. She collected some snow for her precious brew and ate some more of her food. Her food was getting quite low now; would her death be by starvation or freezing? Picking up her bundles she carried on, her breath freezing in the morning air. All day she walked, mile after mile, almost in a dream, until eventually in the distance she could see the last station the train had passed through—Chita.

In a daze she clambered up onto the platform, dropped her luggage and sank down. At first no one took any notice of her. She got out the little folding stool that she had been given by the music teacher. Sitting on that was not so cold as the frozen ground of the platform.

It was now Wednesday 26 October. During the day as Gladys sat huddled against the cold, a man kept coming up and questioning her. He said he could speak English but she could hardly understand a word. The following night she was left with a guard. She put down her improvised bed and for yet another night she tried to make herself as comfortable as she could.

Feeling distressed and frightened, she got out her little pocket Bible. A page from a calendar fluttered out and by the dim station light, she tried to read a further text from Nehemiah.

'Be ye not afraid of them, I am your God.'

Again she felt God speaking directly to her. It was the message she needed to hear at that particular time. She was to remember that text on many occasions during the dark days ahead and able to gain strength from it.

The next day the officials obviously decided that something must be done about this young foreign woman with the battered suitcases. They beckoned her to follow them. By this time her two cases were nearly empty.

It was so cold that she was wearing all the clothes she had with her. The case of food, which had been full twelve days ago, now contained hardly anything.

Two coolies were instructed to pick up her cases for her. Thinking they would be very heavy, they strained to lift them. The next second both of them had turned complete somersaults with the empty cases flying up in the air. In spite of the seriousness of the situation, Gladys laughed and laughed. It was the first time she had laughed since leaving home.

Her amusement, however was short-lived. Her luggage was taken from her and officials examined her passport. They thought the word 'missionary' meant 'machinist.' A skilled factory worker would be most useful in this remote spot. They changed what was written in the passport, although Gladys didn't realise what had happened until later. She was so frightened, she didn't know what to do, so she prayed and gained comfort from God.

She then had an inspiration. She drew out her Bible and showed the officials a little picture text card she had in it. Amazingly, they seemed to understand and issued her with a new visa straight away and a ticket for the next part of her journey.

On Friday, however, she was still in Chita. She had been shown round the town, no doubt to persuade her what a wonderful place it would be to live and work. Eventually her luggage was returned to her and she was put on a train. As far as she could work out, she had to get out at Nikolshissur Junction, take another train from there to Pogranilchnai and then to Harbin. It seemed a very complicated programme to Gladys and in the event it did not work out according to plan.

When Gladys got to Nikolshissur, she was unable to make anyone understand her, so she spent another night on a platform. If anything the cold had intensified and her resistance had lowered. Gladys later remembered this as the second night she thought she would die of cold.

On the morning of the 29th, she had to use every bit of her dogged determination and go looking for a Government Office, where at least she felt someone would speak English. However, she could not make anyone understand her situation and her disappointment was so intense, she was on the verge of tears.

Something made her place her hand in her pocket and bring out a photograph of her brother, Laurence. He was wearing his full dress uniform as a drummer in the British Army. This picture brought tears to her eyes. How far away they all seemed now. Laurence made such a striking contrast to the soldiers around her. He looked tall, alert and upright, posing in his smart uniform. The soldiers with Gladys were down trodden and shabby. Although she could not tell what was being said, she noticed the effect the picture had on her captors. They must have thought they were looking at the picture of a high ranking officer. Their attitude changed immediately.

Before Gladys could catch her breath, they had collected her luggage from the station cloakroom and were escorting her to a hotel. The next day she was put on a train for Vladivostok.

On arrival at Vladivostok station, she was met by a man who took her passport and showed her to an Intourist Hotel. For the first time in many days she was able to hear English spoken.

It was a luxury to have a proper wash at the hotel. She was able to take all her clothes off and have a bath. What luxury. With a change of clothes and a good night's sleep in a proper bed she now felt able to cope with anything. The train journeys had been long and tiring and fraught with danger. She had passed through many time zones and travelled through many countries. She had encountered hardships and deprivations and unable to contact friends and family. There were unknown troubles and trials in the future but the only constant factor in her life was the protection of God.

On the last day of October, feeling refreshed, Gladys was taken on a tour of this cosmopolitan city. Men and women of all nationalities roamed the streets; it was a busy but depressing place, full of dirt and squalor. In every street there were long queues for the black bread, which was sold without being wrapped. The people then sat on the side of the road and ate it. Gladys, who had been brought up to be well-mannered, was horrified. She had never thought there could be sights like this anywhere in the world.

The actual streets themselves were very different from those at home. There were no pavements and the roads had great holes in them. Large puddles had to be circumnavigated or, when it was too dark to see, splashed through.

Chapter 5

As Gladys had to remain in Vladivostok for a few days, she had time to notice that the people here looked different. They had dark skins and tiny eyes and she realised with a shock that they were Japanese. It was heart breaking to see their ragged clothes and thin bodies but they were often carrying fat babies on their backs. As in Russia, the people were carrying great bundles of every kind. More than ever Gladys appreciated the refinements of England.

She prayed constantly, and was able to rejoice that she was going where God wanted her to be.

She next discovered that there would be a problem continuing by train to Harbin. That night in her room, she felt the devil was attacking her and as she read her Bible to gain strength, there was a knock on the door. Opening it slightly, Gladys saw a young girl so heavily attired in winter clothes that her features were indistinguishable.

'You are in great danger. You must get away from here as soon as possible,' she said. 'At first light, an old man will knock on your door. You must follow him.'

And with that she was gone. Gladys sat on her bed shaken and perplexed.

Again there was another knock on her door, more urgent this time. As she opened it a crack she saw it was her interpreter, now a very drunken man. He tried to force his way into her room and Gladys' frail frame was no match for his. Instinctively, she shouted out in English;

'You can't come in here, my God will protect me'

And with that he slunk away.

Gladys couldn't believe it when there was a third knock.

'Who's there?' she cried through the closed door.

'I have your passport.' A male voice said.

Gladys opened the door slightly and made a grab for the passport. She managed to toss it behind her into the bedroom as she hastily slammed the door shut. She was so shaken she hardly slept at all that night and as soon as it started to get light, she heard another knock.

Peering out, she saw an old man standing waiting. Hoping she was doing the right thing, she gathered up her belongings, followed him down the stairs and out into the street.

Weighed down by her luggage, it was hard for Gladys to keep up with the old man, but she followed him until they reached the area of the quayside. There the man disappeared and standing by her side was the girl. She placed her finger on her lips and beckoned to Gladys.

'See that ship over there? It's going to Japan. You must be on it. Speak to the captain and insist he takes you.'

Gladys looked at the old ship tied up by the quayside. Her first thought was that it was China she was trying to reach. Then she realised it was all part of God's plan, and at least Japan was nearer, and maybe safer, than where she was now.

'How can I ever thank you?' Gladys asked.

'Well, have you any spare clothes?'

Because of the cold weather, Gladys knew she was wearing everything she had with her.

'Here, take these gloves,' she took them off her own hands, 'and here is a pair of stockings in my pocket.'

Gladys handed them over and looked at the ship. When she looked back to thank her again, the girl had disappeared. She had been another angel whom God had sent to protect her on her journey.

She approached the hut where the captain was sitting.

Diffidently, she asked,

'Will you please take me to Japan?'

The man looked up. He did not seem surprised, he must have been asked this question many times before.

'Have you any money?'

'No.'

'Then I'll have to take you as my prisoner. Sign here. We are leaving immediately.'

It was so quick and so simple. Gladys was now a prisoner of the Japanese.

As she started to climb the steps into the boat, she was suddenly grabbed from behind, nearly scattering all the bundles. Someone was trying to detain her.

God guided her hand to her pocket. There was the pound she had been given by the Dutch couple long ago and far away. She thrust this into the hand of her attacker and broke free. God had known the trouble she would be facing and had 'gone before'.

Her last trip on a boat seemed so long ago. When she crossed the English Channel she had only just made all her farewells. Now her eyes misted over as she thought of her family. She had been writing notes to them during her journey, but no-one could contact her until she arrived at her journey's end.

Again it was a smooth crossing with beautiful views of the coastline. After three days they arrived at Tsurugaoko and as soon as the ship docked, Gladys found the British Consulate. The officials there did not know what to do with her, until she was able to explain that she needed a train ticket to Kobe. It seemed a complicated journey, but Gladys knew she was getting nearer and nearer her destination.

When the train eventually arrived at Kobe station, Gladys found that she had more confidence, as she knew she was close to people who would be friendly. At the Japanese Evangelical Band Mission Home in Kobe, she knew she would be made welcome. Following enquiries, she had to complete the next part of her journey by rickshaw, a flimsy two-wheeled vehicle, which seemed overcrowded with just herself and her small amount of luggage. By now she was feeling quite ill as the man carrying her trotted along in his wooden shoes, the sounds reverberating over the cobbled ground.

At the mission station, Gladys was made most welcome by Mr and Mrs Dyer. As she arrived she was bowed to and had her shoes, both left ones, removed. Gladys' main thought at this time was that she had a hole in her stocking. She was so embarrassed that she could not remember much about the occasion.

After the meal, in true Japanese style, she was taken to her room. It was such a contrast to what she had been used to for the last few weeks. The white bed was covered by a blue spread, all enhanced by the soft light of a lantern with a red and white shade. Gladys had a wonderful night. She stayed in the care and comfort of the mission for a few days. This short rest strengthened her for the hardships which lay ahead.

On the morning of Saturday 5 November, Mr Dyer was able to obtain a boat ticket from Kobe to Tientsin and she was escorted by her friends down to the steamer. They spoke to the captain, and asked him to look after

Gladys. These memories of Japan were very precious to Gladys; memories that would be sorely tried during future encounters with the Japanese.

Gladys found the eating arrangements rather strange on this ship. Each person was given a little tray with many pots on it. In the pots would be soup, a meat mixture, salad and vegetables, rice and tea. Some she enjoyed, but some she couldn't eat. In her travels towards the end of her life, she would become used to this form of eating, but in the beginning it was unfamiliar to her.

The coastline of Japan looked particularly beautiful as they sailed past. The high mountains were covered with snow, the hills bright green and luxurious with glorious red trees. The Japanese houses clustered in the foot-hills with their quaint roofs and gates hung with flags and banners.

On the Sunday the ship called at the little village of Mogi, about halfway round this picturesque coast line. A man came on board to inspect the passports and he spoke good English, having visited America but not England. What a pleasure it was for Gladys to converse in her own tongue. The man took her ashore to have tea with the high officials and although the tea was horrible, Gladys dutifully drank it. She would soon become used to dining with the important and influential.

The next day the ship sailed away from the coast and the weather became colder. Gladys was finding it harder and harder to remain smart. Her orange dress, which she had worn during so much on the journey, was dirty and torn. She felt worse because the Japanese women were so clean, pretty and petite but her sense of humour bubbled over as she realised, they had not travelled half way round the world in the same clothes.

As the light faded on the 8 November, the captain called Gladys up to the bridge and pointed to the horizon. At first she could see nothing, then her eyes became accustomed to the evening light. Her heart quickened as she followed the direction of his pointing finger. There across the yellow muddy water on the skyline was China. Her heart was full of praise. She was at last looking at the land that would be her home for the next seventeen years.

First impressions of China

Gladys was doubly glad to see China. It wasn't simply that her journey would be over, she was also pleased because ever since she had arrived in Japan, she had to sit cross-legged on the floor and now her back was giving her pain. In China she could sit on a chair again.

On Thursday 10 November the ship landed in China itself. She wrote in her diary that she had arrived at Tientsin at 4.30 am. It was cold and again Gladys had to wear all her warm clothes, though they were looking even more tattered than ever.

She made her way immediately to the missionary society's headquarters. They gave her a tremendous welcome and she was able to stay there a few days.

In her ignorance she had expected Mrs Lawson to be there to meet her, but instead an escort, Mr Lu, had been sent. Jeannie Lawson had moved up into the wild, mountainous country, north of the Yellow River, to a town called Tsehchow. Meanwhile Gladys could enjoy a few days rest after her long journey. On 12 November there was an Armistice Day service at the English church and the service made Gladys think of home. Her family were so far away and she wondered what they were doing. She had written to them, but until she had a permanent address, they would not be able to write back to her.

Her short break was soon over and early the next morning, together with Mr Lu, Gladys started the ninety-mile journey to Peking (now known as Beijing). It was an uncomfortable train journey as each compartment held about thirty or forty people who were jostled about in the lurching carriages. Gladys was glad to know she wouldn't have to use these trains very much.

At first the scenery was flat and uninteresting. The train passed many small mud walled villages. Gladys saw the peasants, still with their pig-tails, driving heavy two-wheeled carts drawn by shaggy Mongolian ponies. The purple mountains in the distance made a beautiful backdrop to the scene.

Shansi was the home of Chinese agriculture and the cradle of Chinese civilization. Crops requiring only minimal rainfall like millet, wheat and barley were grown in abundance.

The night in Peking was her first experience of a Chinese inn. She had expected it to be primitive, but she was still shocked at how basic it was. Besides being very dirty, there was no privacy. Everyone slept on the k'ang, which was a communal brick bed heated from underneath by hot air from the stove. No one undressed and everyone shared the same fleas and lice. It was a new experience for Gladys, but one she would become used to.

The city was full of temples, pagodas, statues and calm lotus-surrounded pools. Gladys needed to buy a pass here, which would allow her to travel inland.

She had very little money left by this time but was trusting God to supply her every need.

Stanley Smith

A further three day journey by train took them to Yutse, a smaller city than Peking. Here they had to leave the train and continue by bus. Gladys marvelled at how narrow the roads were as they meandered round the mountainside. Nothing seemed to deter the driver, who always drove at breakneck speed even through cascading brooks and rivers. Again the journey was uncomfortable for Gladys, who felt the bus shaking her to pieces.

The two day journey from Tientsin to Tsehchow was long and tiring and Gladys was pleased when she arrived. Step by step she was getting near to her destination.

They went straight to the mission, but were disappointed to learn that Mrs Lawson had moved even further up into the mountains, to Yangcheng, a small walled town north of the Yellow River in the province of Shansi. This was a wild area where Christianity had not yet penetrated. Yangcheng was two day's journey away, along the ancient mule-track between Hornan to Hopen.

The mission station at Tsehchow was run by two seventy-year old missionaries. One of the women was a Mrs Smith, widow of Stanley Smith. Gladys was intrigued to hear her story.

Chapter 6

Stanley had come to China in 1885 as one of the 'Cambridge Seven'. These were seven young graduates who, having received the call to China, worked with the China Inland Mission. They had travelled far into the depths of the country preaching the gospel and many came to faith through their ministry.

Stanley Smith had eventually left the CIM for doctrinal reasons and had started his own mission in Eastern Shansi with his headquarters at Tsehchow. He died only shortly before Gladys' arrival, leaving a well-established church and a boarding school. Mrs Smith, who had been an archbishop's daughter, was now in charge of the thriving centre. Gladys took to her immediately. In a letter home, she wrote;

'What a welcome I had. I feel that Mrs Smith is going to be my mother out here. I love her already.'

The other missionary was a lady who found Gladys too informal and casual. Although Gladys didn't know it at the time, this missionary described Gladys as 'a small insignificant woman who arrived in western clothes'.

The western outfit didn't last long!

'You can't travel any longer in those clothes,' said Mrs. Smith 'They make you look like a wealthy woman.'

Gladys had to smile as she thought about the few shillings left in her possession.

'You stand a chance of being robbed in those clothes. I'll give you wadded trousers and a jacket to wear, then you won't be so noticeable.'

Dressed in her new clothes, Gladys' stay in Tsehchow was all too brief and soon she and Mr Lu had to continue their difficult journey. Travelling in traditional Chinese costume was more practical; she now looked like a poor peasant, who would not attract the notice of the bandits who lived in the hills.

The only way now for the couple to travel was by mule, nine miles over the plains and then up the narrow flinty paths of the wild mountains. A canopied platform was secured on to the animal's back and for mile after mile, Gladys had to perch inside, which she found a most uncomfortable mode of transport. She hung on for all she was worth, feeling any moment she would slip off the animal's back and tumble down the mountain-side.

Every bone in her body was shaken and every muscle bruised. As she approached the end of the journey, her destination seemed to be getting further away.

Before dark they had reached Chowtsun, their overnight stop. They needed to be there before nightfall for at dusk the gates were locked and no-one was then allowed to enter. Wolves and bandits made it dangerous. Gladys felt she had so much to learn about the Chinese culture as it was all so different from anything she had ever experienced before.

The next day they continued on their tiring journey. Rushing streams tumbled down the marbled faces of the mountainside, birds of prey flew overhead and the mules' hooves echoed on the flinty track. Seven hours later, Mr Lu stopped the mules and pointed upwards. There like a fairy story castle perched on a hill was their destination, the city of Yangcheng.

Gladys felt like crying for joy. The high walls seemed to grow out of the natural rock. The silhouettes of pagodas and temples pierced the purple sky of the late afternoon. Away behind them fell glorious panoramas of mountains and valleys.

It looked so beautiful.

The noisy hum of the place could be heard from where they were. Everything was so strange. Gladys, still feeling uncomfortable with her strange form of transport, sat gazing at the sight. She was here, the place she knew God wanted her to be.

The city was placed in a strategic position. For many months of the year, mule trains passed daily to and fro. This traffic ceased during the winter when the passes were closed by deep snow. Then everyone remained where they were. Those who were in the city stayed there for the winter and those who had not yet reached it, stayed in the adjacent cities or villages.

This was all so different to Gladys, who had only seen small amounts of snow in London. There was so much she needed to know about the new culture. It was hard to take in all at once.

As the trade route passed right through the city, there were two gates, an East Gate and a West Gate. Travellers entered the city at one gate and exited through the other. Like every mountain city, the gates were locked at night.

As soon as they entered by the East Gate, Gladys knew it was very different from Tsehchow. The roadways were very narrow and dark, with high walls on either side, leading to private courtyards. Mr Lu and Gladys turned left into what proved to be the main street. During the last few days she had been growing used to the strange sights, sounds and smells, but Yangcheng was different.

Here she was receiving hostile stares. The presence of Mr Lu was keeping her safe, but a few men actually picked up stones threatening to throw them at her. Obviously foreigners were treated with suspicion. Her first thought was of desperation, but then she remembered she was about the King's business.

Mr Lu led the mules down the main street, disregarding the unfriendly reactions, and leading her past the dark little shops whose merchandize she could not properly see. He led her past the shoppers, haggling and bartering for their goods and past the children playing and the beggars begging. She saw the long shadows of the temples and heard the hooves of the mules squelching through the mud following recent rain-fall. Gladys was pleased to be safe, high above the mud and away from hostile crowds.

After a hundred yards or so, the track turned into a walled courtyard where, facing them was a dilapidated building. Could this be the end of her journey, Gladys wondered; was this what she had travelled half way round the world to find?

The noise of their mules in the courtyard echoed round the enclosed area and almost immediately a figure came bustling out of the building. The first impression Gladys had was of a short, white haired old lady. She was dressed in a plain blue robe and trousers. Gladys later discovered the reason all clothes were blue was because it was the only dye obtainable from the root of a locally grown plant. Clothed in native dress, the woman before her could have been Chinese, apart from her eyes and white hair.

More than the blue of the clothes, it was the clear blue of her eyes, which riveted Gladys' attention. She radiated energy, her face alert and sharp as she looked up at them. However, the expression on her face was not particularly welcoming.

'And who are you?' she demanded.

Gladys could not believe her ears. Had she come all this way just to be greeted like that?

Start of the Inn

Surely the old woman couldn't have been expecting anyone else, Gladys thought; European visitors couldn't be all that frequent in the city. Showing a spirit she didn't feel, Gladys replied,

'I'm Gladys Aylward and you must be Mrs Lawson.'

'Yes, I am, but come on in. Yang will cook you a bowl of boiled dough strings and chopped vegetables.'

Yang was the Chinese cook and Jeannie's right-hand man. A small, anxious man, he was one of the few locals who was not afraid of the eccentric old lady. He was also a good cook, as Gladys was to find out.

Mrs Lawson seemed confused and had probably forgotten that she'd sent Mr Lu to meet her. Gladys was to learn that Jeannie suffered greatly from mood swings and wasn't always easy to live with. These were characteristics which Gladys herself was to display later in her life.

During the coming months, the younger woman gradually learned her story. It had been a hard life. As Jeannie Arthur, but also known as Jane, she had been born in Scotland in 1860 and had first set sail as a missionary for China in 1887. Two years later she had married Dugald Lawson and had worked in the Shansi province.

For many years Jeannie had suffered ill health and found her furloughs in 1895 and 1900 beneficial. They had both experienced great danger in the anti-Western Boxer uprising which had taken place between the two furloughs. The couple had had five children, but as far as Gladys could learn, Jeannie had buried them all, the fifth after only five day's illness. A few years were spent away from the CIM working in France, but they had finally returned to their original missionary society.

Dugald Lawson had died in the early 1920s while Jeannie was recuperating in Scotland, but now Jeannie herself wanted to die in China with the people who had captured her heart. She had left her own country for the last time, staying a while in Kobe, Japan before finally returning to China and making her base in the mountainous region of Yangcheng. It seemed that Jeannie was the first missionary to work in this area although Gladys was never sure how accurate the whole story was, as Jeannie was apt to be forgetful in her old age.

Once Gladys had settled down, both women tried every way they knew to spread the gospel, but the townsfolk of Yangcheng took little notice, except to abuse them. The people did not listen to them on the streets and would never come into the courtyard of the 'foreign devils.'

However, in spite of her advanced years, Jeannie was a woman of vision. She had a plan. The first part of her plan was to purchase an inn, which she was able to do at a low price, because it was rumoured to be haunted. (The Chinese were very superstitious). Jeannie with her forthright nature, knew she could rely on her God to protect her. She planned to turn the building back into an inn for the muleteers who crowded into the city each evening.

The life of a muleteer was strange to Gladys' western ways. They often had a wife at both ends of the trail, who sent gifts to each other. The regulars stayed at the same inn each time, but there was always a group who had never been to the city before. These would be willing to stay at the first inn that had room for them. It was Jeannie's plan that these men would spend the night in her inn.

Yang, her cook, would prepare the meals for them using millet, maize corn and buck wheat; food they would be familiar with. He would also use a few vegetables, plus pears, peaches and wild dates.

When the muleteers were settled and eating their meals, the plan was for Jeannie to start telling them stories about God from the Bible. The Chinese were an intelligent and receptive people who loved to hear stories. Because they knew their families and friends also loved stories, they would repeat them when they returned home. This would mean the gospel stories would be spread to others without Jeannie and Gladys having to travel at all. Gladys agreed that it was a wonderful way of evangelising and was anxious to do her part in this task.

There was plenty of work for her to do. Being young and strong, she could be responsible for making the inn habitable. She could look after the mules and make sure they were well fed and she could help Yang. Eventually, when she knew Chinese, she could share in the story-telling.

Jeannie thought there would be room for about fifty men to sleep on the k'angs. That would be a guaranteed audience of fifty men who would hear the story of Jesus each night.

Preparing the inn was hard, dirty work. Fortunately for them, the building had originally been intended as an inn, so the layout was ideal, but much renovation was required and the whole place needed a thorough clean. Gladys felt she had never worked so hard in all her life. Although Mrs Lawson had previously suffered ill health, she seemed able to cope with some of the work and was always full of inspirational ideas. She was also a hard task-master; Gladys had to do all the heavy work!

Communication was a problem to Gladys. Being unable to speak Chinese, she could not even go shopping and Yang, the cook, was instructed to teach her. Considering that she had never done well at school, Gladys was a surprisingly quick learner. She learnt by copying what Yang was saying. He went round the kitchen pointing out various items and saying their Chinese name. Although she never achieved a good pronunciation and grammar was unknown to her, Gladys learned quickly. Again her possible dyslexia was a stumbling block, but her alert mind and desire to learn were in her favour. No doubt Gladys had a natural ability; she and her mother had both been skilled in the act of mimicry. This helped her now.

To venture out into the streets was a further adventure. This city had seen few foreigners, and the Chinese were frightened of them. Even Gladys with her dark eyes and hair and short stature was considered a 'foreign devil.' As Gladys went to buy food, she would be pelted with mud and worse. She was shouted at in Chinese and generally shunned.

She became thankful to God for her looks. At only five foot tall, she was of similar stature to many of the Chinese. As a child she'd wished to be taller and longed to have fair hair. As she looked round the inhabitants of the city now, she realised her small frame and dark hair were a great advantage.

Slowly the preparations for the inn were completed. Yang had bought a good supply of millet, maize and vegetables from the market. Jeannie intended their visitors to be well fed. They planned to charge less than other inns in the hope that this would counteract the fact that they were 'foreign devils'.

Jeannie prepared the Bible stories she intended to tell; stories that would be adapted to reflect the Chinese way of life. She couldn't give the impression that Jesus was English.

As each inn displayed its name on the outside, there was a great deal of discussion as to what name they should call theirs. Eventually they decided to call it 'The Inn of Eight Happinesses'. Neither woman knew what happinesses they were listing, but it was a pleasant sounding name and it stuck.

The first night they were to open, there was great excitement. Everything was ready, but Gladys couldn't see how they could persuade muleteers to stop at their inn. Jeannie soon explained her strategy. It would be Gladys' job to drag the lead mule into the courtyard. Once the lead mule was inside, the others would have to follow. Also, as the animals were so tired at the end of the long day, once they were in, nothing would persuade them to leave.

Realising how large and strong the mules were and with a reputation for being temperamental animals, Gladys was dismayed.

'I can't do that', she moaned 'I'm too small and short. I'll be trampled to death.'

'Well I certainly can't do it. I'm too old. You're young and strong.' Jeannie had little patience with her.

'Did I come to China just to deal with mules?' Gladys grumbled to herself.

Now everything was ready, they were excited. Yang had cooked some tasty food in readiness and Jeannie had prepared her Bible stories. It all now depended on Gladys. She had been well briefed by Jeannie and Yang. In her newly acquired Chinese clothes, and sending up hasty prayers to heaven, she stood by the inn wall waiting.

The first evening, she didn't have long to wait. She could hear the pounding, as many mule trains entered the city walls. One by one they stopped at various inns along the road. Gladys called out her greeting as she had been trained.

'Muyo beatcha, muyo goodso, how, how, how, lai, lai lai.'

To her western ears she hoped she was saying, 'We have no bugs, we have no fleas, good, good, good, come, come, come.'

Eventually one train headed her way. The drivers appeared tired and were obviously strangers to Yangcheng for they were peering from side to side looking for accommodation. The mules appeared larger than she remembered and Gladys felt smaller.

As the lead mule drew level with her, she grabbed its harness and pulled and pulled. At first it seemed she was having no impression and the mule train would pass by like many others. However, her strength, combined with the fatigue of the animals, eventually prevailed. The creatures started to stumble into the courtyard.

The muleteers were petrified. They thought their animals were being bewitched by the foreign devils. In a second they had all disappeared and Gladys was left holding the harness.

She stumbled inside and the animals made for the food troughs. There was no sign of the owners and Gladys panicked.

'Jeannie, Jeannie, what shall I do? We've a yard full of animals and no men. What can we do now?'

Alone in the Inn

Jeannie had been praying quietly inside the inn when the noise of the mules and the shouts of Gladys brought her running outside. 'Whatever is the matter, girl?' she asked.

'There are no muleteers and the yard is full of all these animals. What do I do?'

Jeannie smiled. Having more experience of Chinese ways, she knew that no muleteer would leave his animals untended for long. They were worth a lot of money and so was their cargo.

'Don't worry, Gladys, the muleteers won't abandon their animals and goods. They'll soon be back. '

She alerted Yang and resumed her praying. She was right. Before long the men crept back. They were driven by curiosity and hunger. They were not frightened of Yang, the cook. He was one of them. Even Gladys, when they got used to her, wasn't too scary with her black hair and dark eyes. The person that really frightened them most was Jeannie. She had wayward white hair and darted about like a restless bird. No wonder she was known as the 'foreign devil.'

Once they had fed their mules, the men sat down to enjoy their food. And enjoy it they did; Yang was a good cook. There was silence as they ate. It had been a long tiring day. Towards the end of the meal they found themselves listening to stories, gospel stories. Jeannie was a born story-teller.

They heard how Noah had escaped from the flood. They knew all about floods for many of them had witnessed the flash floods that had rushed down the mountain valleys. Some of them had even lost mules or friends in them. They heard the story of Joseph and as most of them had brothers, they knew all about jealousy. David, the shepherd they could identify with, for they often risked their lives for their animals.

They heard the stories of Jesus. That was a puzzle to them. How could there be a God who loved them enough to die for them? Their mountain gods were not like that.

Night after night the stories were told as seven or eight different mule teams spent their evenings at the inn. Day after day the story of the gospel was repeated up and down the mountain cities. The Good News was spreading.

When Yang had finished his cooking it was his turn at story telling. The only snag was that he loved Noah and brought him into every story. According to him Noah was with Jesus in Jerusalem, with Moses in Egypt and with Paul in Rome!

Gladys longed to take her turn at telling the stories. She was a quick learner, but Chinese was an extremely difficult language. Furthermore, different areas had different dialects and in the market place she could hear them all. She was impatient. At first she could only tell a few stories, but she improved. She smiled when she thought about the Bible college who had rejected her as too old to learn Chinese.

Gladys also waited impatiently to be accepted. For months she watched and waited. Then one day, in the market place, she heard herself referred to as

'Ai-weh-deh'. Apparently Yang couldn't manage the name Aylward, and in any case Gladys needed a Chinese name. Jeannie had decided she should be know as 'Ai weh -deh',

'Yang, what does Ai-weh-deh mean?' she asked.

'Virtuous one,' replied Yang.

That was enough for Gladys, she knew she had been accepted. It was a name she was proud to keep all her life.

Gladys discovered that she and Jeannie didn't have a great deal in common. Firstly, Jeannie came from the Highlands of Scotland and Gladys had never even travelled as far as the north of England. Secondly, Jeannie was over seventy, with the wisdom of someone of that age whereas Gladys was in her early thirties, and although she needed to defer to Jeannie in most matters, she didn't find it easy. Also Jeannie was short tempered and intolerant and Gladys had the same characteristics. Clashes were inevitable. The only thing that held them together was a desire to serve God.

Yang was the great peace-maker. He often advised Gladys to keep out of the way when Jeannie lost her temper. She would go to the market and usually by the time she returned, it had all blown over. On one occasion

Jeannie shouted and screamed at Gladys over a very small incident and told her to return to England. The atmosphere was so bad that Gladys decided to return to the neighbouring city for a while and stay with the missionaries there, Dr and Mrs Hoyte.

This wasn't the first time she had been with them. She loved their children and they loved her. She was also useful in looking after them if their parents had to go away for a short while. This time she stayed longer with the family.

While she was there caring for the children, a messenger came from Yangcheng. Gladys was full of foreboding. What had happened?

'The white devil. She dies. Come, come, quickly.'

It was a garbled message. Gladys couldn't understand. Jeannie had been fine when she had left her, just cross. Gladys left the children in the care of neighbours and made the journey back to Yangcheng. Here the news was also confused.

It appeared Jeannie had gone trekking over the hills to the neighbouring town of Chin Shui. There she had gone up to the balcony of a house, leaned on the banister, which was rotten, and fallen on to the courtyard below

Gladys gathered together such medical supplies she could, and with the messenger, journeyed up to the remote village of Chin Shui.

She was appalled by what she found.

When Jeannie had fallen she had been moved to a barn full of coal and then left lying on the ground. The villagers were afraid of this devil and would not touch her. They gave her some water but were not willing to give food to a person that was about to die.

Gladys screamed and shouted at them to get Jeannie to a place of safety. In the relative comfort of the inn she tended Jeannie's wounds which were severe and gently washed her face which was still caked in the blood from the fall.

Jeannie was delirious and for about six weeks lay with her back badly injured.

When she showed no signs of improving, Gladys arranged for her to be carried back to Yangcheng.

This was a treacherous journey for one so ill. The mountain passes were steep and dangerous. On more than one occasion the bearers nearly fell.

There was still no improvement in Jeannie's condition and Gladys felt sure she was dying. She then got Jeannie on to a mule and with the help of men from the village, transported her to the hospital at Luan, six days journey away.

Yang was left in charge of the inn and no doubt continued telling his Bible stories in which Noah figured so strongly. Everything was done to save Jeannie, but to no avail. On 23 November 1933, aged seventy-four, Jeannie Lawson the Scottish missionary died.

Gladys remembered that she had often found Jeannie difficult to get along with, due to the difference in their age and upbringing. Gladys smiled as she realised she wasn't always easy to get along with herself. She had to admit that the one thing she had learned from Jeannie, was how to pray and praying was what she needed most to do now.

Gladys had been in China less than a year and now she was alone. It would be hard for Gladys and Yang to carry on alone with the inn. What would they do for money? Jeannie's pension had stopped with her death. As Gladys stood worrying, she looked at the text hanging on the wall of her room.

'Be not afraid, I will be with you.'

The future was known to God, though not to Gladys.

The funeral service was attended by many people who had come to love her and had come to believe in her God. The people of Yangcheng had been won over by the care and concern of this 'foreign devil'.

Among the mourners was Hsi Lien, one of the very first muleteers to be persuaded to stay at the inn. Gladys was pleased he could be there. Hsi Lien had become a Christian, one of their first converts. However, if Gladys had been able to see into the future, she would have wished that Hsi Lien and his family had left Yangcheng and never returned. His faith would one day result in his family facing a terrible death, the trauma of which would eventually send him insane.

Foot inspector

With the overthrow of the Ch'ing Dynasty in 1912, there had been a more relaxed attitude in China. Except for the priests and important men, fewer were wearing queues, (the long pigtails that reached half way down their backs). Now there was a change coming for the women.

Apparently, many years ago, one of the wives of a previous Emperor had escaped from the palace. It had been argued that if the girl's feet had been restricted, she would not have been able to run at all, so from that time, the appalling habit of binding little girls' feet had begun. As their bones were soft at birth, the toes were curled under towards their soles and bound together. This meant the feet would stay bent and walking was almost impossible.

Gladys had become used to seeing the women shuffle round on their tiny feet and could see the pain etched on their faces. Now all this was to change; it was decreed by law that this barbaric practice was to stop. When babies were born, their feet were to remain free.

It was not a reform that happened quickly. Many husbands were opposed to it and wives were afraid to disobey their husbands. In the larger cities, babies' feet were unbound quite quickly, but in the outlying villages, like Yangcheng, the law was more difficult to enforce. It was the responsibility of the Mandarin in each district to implement the change.

Gladys hardly knew her local Mandarin and was therefore in awe of this distant potentate. One day, she received a summons to visit him. She asked Yang what the protocol was for visiting such a person but he was no help.

'Woman and foreigners do not visit the Mandarin.'

'But, Yang, he has summoned me to visit him. I must go.'

So there was no precedent. The Mandarin was the mayor, ruler and judge of Yangcheng and was to be obeyed. Not knowing what to do, Gladys did nothing, hoping the problem would go away, but it did not.

One morning while Gladys was at prayer, she heard an excited cry from Yang,

'The Mandarin's coming! The Mandarin's coming!'

Gladys hurried down the stairs and was amazed by what she saw. A magnificent sedan chair, held by four coolies, was being carried into the courtyard. The velvet curtains were drawn, hiding the person inside. Around the sedan chair were grouped, what Gladys later learned, were the Mandarin's clerks, dressed in deep blue robes. Behind them were learned-looking men with long beards. The whole scene was like one of the films Gladys used to watch so far away in England.

As the coolies stopped, one of the clerks pulled back the curtains and out stepped a tall elegant figure. What a spectacle! His ivory coloured face was completed by a long dark beard. A magnificent black queue hung down from his skull cap and his scarlet flowing robes reached down to his pointed shoes. He stood looking down at Gladys with dark impenetrable eyes.

She bowed. She didn't know what else to do. She bowed again.

'Do you know it is now illegal to bind the feet of baby girls?' he demanded.

'Yes.' Gladys couldn't think what interest it could possibly be to her or why the Mandarin should visit her just to impart this information.

'It's my responsibility to get rid of this evil practice in my province. You must find me someone who will visit the outlying villages to insist this law is kept. No male is allowed to look at a woman's naked foot, so none of my officials can do the job.'

'But I don't know of anyone.'

'Of course you must. There are mission stations all over China.'

Gladys felt this was an exaggeration, but promised to do what she could. She watched as the stately procession swept out of the courtyard. She wrote letters to her few contacts, explaining the pay was a measure of millet and a farthing a day, not exactly a fortune.

After two months Gladys received no encouraging replies and the day she dreaded arrived. The Mandarin returned.

'Have you found anyone to do the job?'

'No sir, women from other provinces cannot live on millet, they are used to rice and no-one is willing to travel on a mule.'

'Then you must do the job.'

Gladys could not believe her ears. She had come to China as a missionary, not as a Mandarin's employee. Her job was to preach the gospel, not to inspect feet. Then suddenly a thought occurred to her—she could preach as she inspected feet.

Gladys looked down at her own feet. She had never thought much about them before. At size three, she'd always thought they were quite small. She wriggled her toes freely in the Chinese cloth-made shoes she wore. The soles were made from the bark of a tree and sometimes only lasted about two weeks before wearing out. Gladys had twelve or more pairs made at a time. This was such a contrast to the footwear of her own country.

'If I'm to do this job and visit the villages, I shall expect to preach about my God to the people.'

'I don't care what you do so long as you unbind the feet. My soldiers will go with you to protect you and make sure you are obeyed.'

With a magnificent sweep he was back inside his sedan chair and gone.

How Gladys rejoiced that night in her prayers. God had provided her with money she so much needed and a means of preaching the gospel. She felt humbled by the fact that she had been so frightened about the future. She had not known how she would manage without Jeannie but God had provided for her.

'Foot Inspector to the Mandarin.' The title had an important ring about it. Gladys didn't know then that she would be doing this work for a number of years, in fact it would be her job until she had to leave Yangcheng itself.

She found the job carried a mark of respect. For the first time Yang showed her deference. He took to bowing to her when he walked into the room, until Gladys asked him to stop doing it. When she walked round the market, people no longer shunned her or threw missiles at her but showed her respect. No human could have planned it so well.

Travelling on her mule, with the soldiers to protect her, Gladys was able to travel to distant villages and hamlets in the mountains. Although she enjoyed the spectacular scenery, she also enjoyed meeting the people. It wasn't long before she came to know the five dialects spoken in the province.

The women were usually working in their courtyards or shyly peeping out from their simple homes. At first they were frightened of her and stopped spinning their thread or winnowing the grain as they eyed her suspiciously. As well as stopping the practice of foot-binding, Gladys also had to tell them about the evils of opium smoking. A visit from this foreigner could be life-changing for these village women.

At first they would not let her approach their children, fearing she might cast an evil spell on them. The women were also afraid of their husbands who were not in favour of what Gladys was doing. Then in one village, an old lady came forward and asked Gladys to unbind her feet. Gladys shook her head sadly, it was many years too late for this old woman to walk properly, however, her initiative gradually encouraged the mothers to approach Gladys.

Slowly they began to accept her and she was able to gain the trust of the young children and unbind their feet. Gladys' heart went out to the young girls who were too old to have their feet unbound; their feet were crippled forever. The older women were also maimed, but for the babies she could bring relief.

As she gained their confidence, she told them the stories of Jesus. On her journeys, she had plenty of time for prayer and this gave her strength for the demands on her life. She wrote in her Bible that prayer wasn't an exercise, it was life itself.

As she unbound the children's feet she explained that as she was freeing the children's feet, God could free the souls. Many accepted the gospel gladly and rejoiced in the double freedom.

It was in her journeys that Gladys learned the hill dialects which would be so useful to her in the future. She made friends with the women she met; especially, a young widow with three young children, called Ru Mai. This woman learned to trust Gladys and began to help her in the work. Eventually Ru Mai was able to take over the work at the inn while Gladys went on her travels. In years to come they were to share many adventures and trials together, which in this happy period they would never have imagined.

Back at the inn, Yang was a great help to her, but his confusion over the Bible stories meant the muleteers were often getting the stories wrong. This worried Gladys, but God had heard her prayer. Help was at hand. Mrs Smith back at Tsehchow was able to send over a young convert, Lu Yung, to help with the work.

In spite of this, Gladys felt lonely. She was so far from England and news took a long time to reach her. She knew she was where God wanted her to be, but she was still lonely. Gladys wanted to be a missionary with a husband and often prayed that this might happen. In her fertile mind she imagined a prospective husband riding over the mountains to come and claim her, just like they did in films.

In the absence of a husband, Gladys prayed for a fellow missionary to work with her. On two occasions there were plans for someone to join her, but each time they fell through. However, God had other more startling plans for her.

Front row from left: Elder Chin, David and Jean Davies and Gladys Aylward

Motherhood

After two years in China, Gladys was returning from one of her villages, when she was approached by a beggar woman, dressed in faded clothes, with silver earrings and necklace. The green puttees round the bottom of her baggy trousers showed she didn't come from Yangcheng. As she got nearer to Gladys, she thrust a bundle towards her and offered it for two dollars.

Gladys peered at it and was shocked to see it was a baby. Gladys guessed it was a girl as baby girls were of no use in Chinese society and were often given away for small sums of money.

What could she do with a baby? She had more than enough to do with foot inspections and running the inn. There was no place for babies in her life. She wanted to refuse, but hadn't quite got the heart to do so. She felt in her pocket and as usual found she had hardly any money at all.

'I can't buy her,' Gladys said 'I've only got ninepence on me.'

'That's enough.' The women grabbed the money, thrust the bundle into Gladys' arms and hurried away down the road. It transpired she had stolen the baby in order to earn a little money. She knew she would be in trouble if she were discovered and thought the foreigner would be a soft touch.

Gladys made enquiries in the area, but no-one claimed the dirty bundle of a child. After a good bath and much tender loving care, the baby was made presentable and began to thrive. Much later Gladys found out that the child had been christened Mei-en, meaning Beautiful Grace. Gladys called her 'Ninepence', the price she had paid for her. 'Ninepence' was the first of Gladys' family.

As the baby grew and became a small child, she said to Gladys one day: 'For my dinner can I have a little less and will you have a little less?'

This was most unusual as Ninepence enjoyed her food. Gladys enquired why.

'Well, there's this little boy out in the street and he's got no dinner at all. Can we put our two lesses in a bowl so he can have a meal?'

Gladys could not refuse. The little boy was given a good meal and remained with them for had nowhere else to go. When Gladys came to giving him a name, she decided it had to be 'Less.' Old enough to tell his story, Less told how bandits had raided his village in Horbag; the men were killed, the women taken off. Less' mother had been pregnant so she was left behind. Less had watched her die in agony and then wandered round the mountains begging for food.

The next children to join the family were Francis and Lan-Hsiang. During the winter, the Yellow River had flooded its banks. Many families had become refugees and fled to the higher mountainous areas; many had drowned. These two children were orphans and had no-one to care for them and so they were brought to Gladys, who could not turn them away.

Another child, 'Dusty Heap' was named after the place where she had been found. The existing family had wonderful ideas for naming its new members.

In the spring of the following year, Gladys was on the river bank doing her washing, in true Chinese style, by pounding her quilted garments with a piece of wood. Suddenly Ninepence and Less came up holding the hands of a two year old.

'Take him back to his parents at once,' said Gladys crossly.

'But we just found him. He had no-one with him,' the children explained.

'But he can't have suddenly appeared.'

'He did. We were playing and looked and saw him. We didn't see anyone put him there.'

Gladys put up notices asking for the child's parents to come and claim him, but no one came, so Bao-bao had joined their family. Then the Mandarin gave to Gladys another child, who had been found with no-one to care for him. As the number of children increased, so did the need for schooling. The prison governor had three children of his own, which increased the number of children needing education. Eventually the Mandarin intervened and a small school was formed.

It was another five years before Gladys learned about Ninepence. Less reported one day that a man had been following Ninepence about. Gladys alerted the Mandarin and it was arranged for soldiers to guard her. When the man was caught he was put in prison; he was an agent for the child's uncle. Ninepence's father had died and the mother was married off, but then sadly died. Ninepence as a female child was not wanted and had been given to a child dealer. The grandparents had then died leaving a farm and money to the uncle and Ninepence. The uncle now wanted to kidnap Ninepence and claim her share of the money.

In the end Gladys had to go to court to claim responsibility for the child. Fortunately the Mandarin was in charge of the court and instructed her only to say 'Yes' or 'No'. It was decided that Gladys would be the official guardian of Ninepence and could then choose the inheritance in either land or the money. Land was of no use to a Chinese girl, so Gladys chose the money. Eventually, this money went towards Ninepence's education and then for her dowry.

Gladys became very friendly with Mrs Smith, the widow of Stanley Smith from Tsehchow. They did not often have time to see each other, but they met whenever they could. Mrs Smith was by now quite elderly, and in 1934 when she came to stay with Gladys, she was taken ill. Although Gladys tended her carefully, Mrs Smith eventually died at the Inn of the Eight Happinesses. Gladys felt even more alone now. How she longed for Western companionship. First Jeannie had died and now Mrs Smith.

Gladys was delighted when, a year later, the Smiths were replaced by David and Jean Davies. Jean, who came from Perthshire, later described Gladys as 'a wee thin thing with great dark staring eyes.' They were sent out by their mission society to work in Tsehchow.

David Davies, then aged thirty-three, was a Welshman who had lived in China before. After the First World War he had worked in the International Customs. He was a brave God-fearing man, who had felt distressed about the illegal trafficking of guns that was taking place on his part of the River Yangtse. He was not prepared to receive any arms and on one occasion confiscated the cargo of a ship bound up-river.

The Communists were an unforgiving people and three days before his tour of duty was to end, they captured David and informed him he would be executed the following day. He witnessed the head of a fellow Chinese prisoner being cut off, but about the same time a British merchant ship came into view. A gun battle then ensued between the British ship and those involved with the gun-running. In the confusion, David escaped and lay low for three days.

He returned to England, but the ignorance and poverty in China had affected him, so he went back with his wife, Jean and son Murray, but this time as a missionary. Their journey was eventful.

The three travelled by train to Pao Ai Hornan, a city to the south of the Yellow River. They then continued north by mule through the mountainous area to Tsehchow. It was arranged that their luggage would follow. When it didn't, David returned to the Yellow River to see what was the matter.

Having located their belongings, David began the return journey alone. Unfortunately he was attacked by bandits, who took all his baggage and then threatened to kill him. They could not decide whether to use him as a ransom or kill him and dispose of his body. God, however intervened. They suddenly let him go, but although his life was saved, all the belongings which the couple had collected back in England, were gone.

Gladys was delighted to have fellow countrymen living near-by, even if it was two day's journey away. Jean and Gladys became great friends and they shared many experiences together. After Paul and little Ruth had been born into the family, Gladys would help with the children whenever she could. Back in 1934 none of them knew the cost of their friendship. None of them could know the influence that Gladys' actions would have on all their lives.

In spite of all the difficulties, Gladys always knew God had called her to work in China, but she felt she needed a stronger sense of belonging. She didn't want to be like some of the missionaries she had heard of, who lived comfortable Western lives while still on the mission field. She wanted to live with the people, to suffer with them and if necessary give her life for them. She wanted to be completely one with them.

With this thought in mind, during the 1930s she decided to destroy her English passport. In 1935 she was granted a certificate of Chinese citizenship from the Ministry of the Interior. Gladys never did things by half; if she made up her mind to do something, she did it and by doing this she could no longer rely on the protection of the British Government. She was now a naturalised Chinese. If she could have known the far-reaching consequences this move was to have, she might have hesitated.

Justice in China

In spite of living in China for many years, the fact remained that Gladys had been brought up in a different culture and the ways of the Chinese sometimes appalled her. The horror of the first execution she witnessed would stay with her for a long time.

Out shopping in the market one day, she was surprised to see many people crowding the streets of Yangcheng and all going in the same direction. This was something she hadn't experienced before. Ever curious, she followed. Maybe a travelling musician was visiting the town or someone of great importance. She followed the crowd to a hill just outside the city gates.

Working her way to the front, she saw a man kneeling on the ground, his hands tied behind his back and his head bent. Before she had time to register what was happening and tear her eyes away, an official standing in front of the man raised his sabre in the air. Gladys could feel what was going to happen but was unable to move a muscle. The sabre was lowered. Still warm, the prisoner's head rolled into the crowd who cheered loudly. Gladys left this barbaric scene and ran to the inn crying. Yang and Lu Yung tried to explain that this man had been a thief and murderer so he deserved to die. This was Chinese justice, but at first she was inconsolable.

Remembering her English history, she knew that Charles I and many others, had been beheaded and that hoards of Londoners had flocked to witness the spectacle. She still felt she had witnessed an equally barbaric act here in China. The shock of witnessing this first execution haunted her for a long time.

The prison in Yangcheng was an unknown place to Gladys. As a woman, she never had occasion to visit it and she never gave it a thought, until the day she was forced to go inside herself.

She was quietly going about her own business, when she received a summons from the Mandarin. Since his first visit, when she had become his Foot Inspector, she had often gone to his court-yard to see him. Both the Mandarin and Gladys had sharp minds and they enjoyed discussions together. They came from different cultures, were the opposite sex, varied in age, but they both enjoyed their meetings. The Mandarin was not used to a women standing up to him. She could argue as skilfully as he could and sometimes she got her own way.

The Mandarin had now sent for Gladys again. As she entered his court-yard, she stood before the scarlet-robed figure, with high collar, scarlet cap and wide-sweeping sleeves. Gladys had no idea what he wanted this time. After the customary greetings, so essential in Chinese culture, the Mandarin came to the point.

'Ai-weh-deh, there's a riot in the prison. The prisoners are killing each other.'

'I'm sorry to hear that, but it's nothing to do with me.'

'I want you to go in and stop it.'

'Me! How can I stop it? I'm only a woman. Send in the prison warders.'

'There're too frightened. It will be fine for you. You've always said your God would take care of you.'

Gladys wished then she'd been a bit less vocal in praising her God, but then she stopped and recalled how often God had taken care of her; during the frozen night in Siberia, in Japan and at the inn in Yangcheng God had provided her with an income as the Foot Inspector. Yes, God would take care of her. To refuse to do this would be to deny his deity. The Mandarin would think her God was as ineffectual as his own gods were proving to be. She had to defend his name.

Confidence in God did not take away her fear. As she drew near to the prison, she could hear the blood-curdling yells and terrified screams. The governor had told her that one of the prisoners had got hold of an axe and had already killed two other men. It now sounded as if more were to follow. She had heard about the conditions inside and knew the prisoners were desperate men. They seldom had enough to eat and had nothing to do—in fact most of them stayed in the prison for many years and some died in there. Attacks and fights were not unusual.

What could a five-foot tall, Englishwoman do against something like this?

In God's strength she drew near to the prison gate. As the key was turned Gladys was praying hard.

She stepped inside and the door slammed shut behind her. Alone and in the dark passage, her fear increased as she moved down the tunnel into the prison courtyard. The sight that met her was appalling. Groups of prisoners were ranged round the walls, some tending their injuries, others were trying to hide but there was no place to hide. Two bodies lay in a pool of blood in the centre of the yard.

Roaring round the place and lunging at groups of men was the prisoner with the axe. Gladys saw to her dismay that he was a large man. His hair was unkempt and in disarray while his tattered prison uniform was liberally splattered with blood. Gladys looked into his eyes; they were blood-shot and wild. She shuddered as the forces of light met the forces of dark.

Trying to avert her attention from the bodies at her feet, Gladys stepped forward and looked straight into his eyes. He took a lunge forward waving his axe aloft. Her eyes never left his face. Slowly and deliberately, Gladys held out her hands.

The courtyard was still. No one moved. Gladys took a deep breath before she said in a firm voice in her clearest Mandarin dialect;

'Give it to me.'

The prisoners stood still, waiting. The officials outside stood still, waiting. The birds out on the mountainside seemed to pause in their flight, waiting.

'Give it to me.'

Mad eyes stared at her as the axe was raised yet again, but she continued to stand there resolutely. Slowly and hesitantly the axe was lowered and equally slowly, placed in her outstretched hands.

Gladys quickly passed it to the officials outside and turned to face the prisoners. When she asked them what their grievances were, she was bombarded with tales of woe. Most men never expected to be set free and they had nothing to do, little chance of exercise and were starving hungry.

As Gladys left the prison she thought about their plight and tried to devise a solution. The next day she requested an audience with the Mandarin and after the usual formal greetings, Gladys started to outline the problems and suggested ways to resolve them.

'That riot started because of the poor conditions in the prison.'

'Nothing can be done about that.'

'Yes, it can. They need better food and more exercise.'

'And where is the money coming from, to buy the food.'

'The men will earn the money.'

'Earn money? How?'

Gladys had given the matter plenty of thought and prayer.

'They can be set to work. Looms can be brought into the prison so they can weave their own clothes. This will be better than their rotting prison rags. They can also breed and sell rabbits. Provide a grindstone, then the men can grind their own grain to produce their own food. There's a few ideas for a start.'

The Mandarin, who was becoming used to Gladys' wild ideas, agreed with her suggestions. He had been concerned about the state of this prison for a long time, but had been unable to see a way out of the problem. Gradually, conditions did in fact improve for the prisoners.

Gladys also found time in her busy schedule to visit and preach to the prisoners. Although their conditions were still harsh, a number eventually became converts to the gospel and they never forgot it was Gladys who had brought about the changes.

Gladys became very fond of one particular prisoner named Hsing, whose name meant 'Star'. When he arrived in the prison he had a white rabbit, which he gave to Gladys to look after. He was exceptionally sad because he was shackled to an older man and both prisoners were therefore restricted in their movements.

In time both men came to trust in Christ and they both prayed for their chains to be removed. They knew it was a direct answer to prayer when this did happen and they were actually unshackled. Gladys gave a gospel to Hsing, but while he slept, the rats ate through it. Gladys then gave him another gospel and a tin to keep it in. The two men then requested if they could hold a small service together and Gladys was then able to give them two Bibles and two hymnbooks. The prison was indeed becoming a different place.

A few months later, a Christian friend of the prison governor, came to preach at Gladys' mission. Gladys saw this as a wonderful opportunity and she approached the governor;

'I think your prisoners should have a chance to hear your friend preach.'

'Certainly, Ai-Wei-Deh,' said the governor, 'I'll arrange for him to visit the prison one day.'

'No,' said Gladys, 'I want them to hear him at the Inn of the Eighth Happinesses.'

'But if we let them out of prison, they'll escape.'

'How can they escape with great chains tied to their legs? In any case, I'll tell them not to.'

So great was the governor's trust in Gladys that he agreed to allow them to come to the inn. In spite of her confidence, Gladys was still relieved that no prisoner did try to escape and they all heard the visiting speaker.

No-one knew then, least of all Gladys herself that in a few year's time, she would be asked to buy some of these very prisoners.

Chapter 12

War

W ars had been part of life in China since the earliest times, both civil war and wars with other nations. While Gladys had been in Yangcheng there had been fighting and rumours of war, but they did not affect her day to day life. Yangcheng and the province of Shansi were mountainous and although on the mule trails, the area was of little interest militarily. The hillside villages were neither aware nor interested that Chu The and Mao Tse Tung were marching along the Manchurian border towards Luan in the north with the Eighth Route Army and that the Japanese were also massing their troops.

Until now the only war these Chinese had known had been inter-tribal skirmishes but all this was to change one sunny morning in 1938.

Early, before the time of prayer, Gladys had been looking out at the surrounding mountains. They looked so peaceful, bare and high above the skyline, scarred with the narrow, flinty mule tracks.

These mountains saw deep snows in winter and wild flowers blossoming along the river banks in the spring. They were bisected with sparkling streams, running fast over dark stones where the Chinese women washed their clothes. It was a peaceful and timeless picture.

On this particular morning, the townspeople of the city were going about their daily business, visiting the market place, cleaning, bartering, spinning, weaving and caring for their families. At about ten o clock, Ru Mai, Lu Yung and Gladys began their daily prayer time. There was so much to pray for; the people were in need materially and spiritually. Suddenly over the sound of their prayers, they heard a distant droning of advancing planes. Gladys knew exactly what was happening; having been in London during the First World War. Now war had arrived in Yangcheng. No one moved, but Gladys prayed,

'Lord, protect us, you are over and above these planes and their evil intentions.'

Out in the streets all eyes were turned skywards and the people saw a sight they had never seen before. Small silver birds were flying straight towards them. They looked so pretty as they grew larger in the sky. It was like a visitation from another planet. They were still standing in the streets gazing upwards as the Japanese aircraft dropped their bombs.

Gladys had once described the people of China as simple-minded, guileless and peace-loving. This may have been the case before this momentous day, but the air raid changed things for ever. The people of Yangcheng didn't stand a chance. Many who were hit with the bombs were killed outright while others were seriously injured. Buildings collapsed trapping those who were inside.

The Inn did not escape. One bomb hit the kitchen and another hit one of the guest rooms. Fortunately no one was in it at the time. The men's room above the kitchen was completely destroyed and the whole roof was reduced to piles of debris. Gladys was knocked unconscious as the ceiling and walls caved in.

The Chinese were panicking as they ran to and fro, not knowing what to do or where to go. The first thing Gladys remembered was hearing Yang and others frantically clearing the rubble so she could be gradually pulled free. Once conscious, Gladys examined her cuts and bruises, and realised she was not badly hurt. She then looked around and was dismayed by what she saw.

A dust hung over the city from the fallen masonry. Rubble was lying everywhere and groups of people were trying to free those who were trapped. Wailing and moans could be heard everywhere. As had so often been the case before, her organizing powers were invaluable. The injured and dying needed her attention.

Glancing briefly at the lopsided text still hanging on a shattered wall, 'I can do all things through God who strengthens me' she grabbed an inadequate medicine box, and began tending the wounded and organising the clear-up. What she could not do herself she persuaded others to do.

She bound up those who had only sustained minor injuries and then sent them to help others. She then organised the clearing of the main street for nobody could be helped while that was blocked. She used part of the Inn that was still intact, to house the wounded. In another section she laid out the dead.

The people of Yangcheng in their confused state, thought a spy in their midst must have told the enemy where they were. They couldn't grasp the fact that the Japanese were bombing other cities in an attempt to conquer the whole of the country. They had so little knowledge of life outside their own region.

Chian Pau, the man they singled out as the supposed spy, was one of Gladys' converts. He had the care of his wife, mother, two small children with another on the way. Gladys did all she could to intervene on his behalf, but no-one would listen to her. When it came to their law, no foreigner could interfere.

'You go and find a Chinese gentleman to stand with you,' she was told.

But everyone was afraid. No one was willing to be connected with a 'spy'. While she was still trying to gain support she heard the crowd's roar as Chian Pau was beheaded.

Gladys felt her heart was broken. All she could do now was to take his family into hiding for fear of further reprisals. She hid them for three days and then took them to Ching Cheng.

Gladys had lost nearly all her possessions. All that remained were two planks for a bed, two stools and a basin. Anything else that had survived the attack had been looted. Food was becoming difficult to obtain, and Gladys was often hungry. Even the staple foods, millet and maize, were not always obtainable, so she was sometimes reduced to eating spring weeds picked straight from the ground.

Frightened of further attacks, the people began to leave the city and hide in the mountains. In the hills there were also Chinese soldiers, but one could not always tell which side they were on. Gladys took the injured to the hillside village of Bei Chai Chuang (Peh Chia Chuang) where they were nursed in mountain temples and caves. She then returned to escort the family of the supposed spy from Ching Cheng to Tsechow where she felt they would be safer. After this she returned to Yangcheng, but then discovered her own life was in danger.

David Davies had received a message to say that Japanese soldiers were advancing on Yangcheng. For Gladys, who had just returned there, it was too late for her to return to Tsechow. She wandered round the city which now seemed deserted, and was overcome by a great sadness. This place she loved and where she had lived so long, was badly damaged. Walking into the Inn, she picked up a text lying on the floor, 'God has chosen the weak things.'

Feeling very weak and vulnerable, she took comfort in this verse. She was certainly weak, but God was strong and he would still protect her. She stayed longer than she intended, reminiscing.

She suddenly heard the sound of advancing soldiers at the East Gate. Her means of escape was cut off. Hurrying to the West Gate, she slipped through it and down to the cemetery beyond. Attempting to escape, she hid behind graves and vegetation but a number of shots were fired, one of which knocked her off her feet and injured her shoulder. The lack of opportunity to tend to her wound, was to cause her much trouble later in her next bid for freedom.

She managed to reach the village of Chin Shui and continued caring for those who needed her. She remained hidden there for a further two months, avoiding the Japanese, in the safety of her mountain home.

Not all her converts were so fortunate. Hsi-Lien, one of the first muleteers to come to faith, who had also been present at the graveside of Jeannie Lawson, was captured by the Japanese in his home. When they realised he was young and strong, they ordered him to carry ammunition for the army.

'I can't,' he replied fearfully. 'I'm a Christian. I don't believe in fighting.'

'Then we'll show you what we do to people who don't co-operate with us.'

Hsi-Lien was prepared to die for his faith, but what happened next was far worse.

The Japanese tied him to a post outside his home. They then locked his wife and three children inside the building and set fire to it. Hsi-Lien had to endure their dying screams as he watched helplessly.

When he was finally released, he staggered to the village where Gladys was hiding. He was so incoherent with grief, that it was a while before she could make out what had happened. After that, she kept Hsi-Lien with her, but his distress was so great, that he eventually lost his mind and went completely insane.

It was probably about this time that Gladys wrote home to her family on a grubby piece of paper. Her words seemed to echo Naomi's daughter-in-law, Ruth, 'Do not wish me to be out of this situation, for I will not leave while this trial is on. These are my people. I will not desert them. God had given them to me and I will live or die with them to his honour and his glory.'

Further war

News from Gladys took a long time to reach England. Her anxious mother, was often interviewed by the local press. Extracts appeared in the local Edmonton newspapers about the progress of this little missionary. At one time Gladys told her mother about the advancing Japanese armies that were only four days away, but by the time Rosina knew about it, that danger was past and another one was looming.

When the Japanese were no longer in the city, the Mandarin called together the dignitaries of the city for a meeting. It was unknown for a woman to attend these meetings, but on this occasion, Gladys was invited.

She looked round for what was to be the last time. She had spent many happy hours here, discussing matters with the Mandarin but that was all in the past.

The officials looked tired and tattered. They knew it was the end for their city. Yangcheng had changed hands four times. Life would never be the same again. The last meal together was served with sad tradition and at the end of it, the Mandarin had an announcement to make. Gladys couldn't imagine what he had to say. The room fell silent.

'In honour of all that Ai-wei-deh has done for us, I wish to become a Christian.'

Gladys was amazed. In the past they had had many discussions about their gods. She hoped he really understood what he was doing. Perhaps she really was being used to spread the gospel more than she had thought.

Many practical things had to be decided at this meeting. One was the problem of releasing the prisoners who could not just be left to the mercy of the Japanese. Those who had families were returned home after being bought back for a fee. Gladys was responsible for escorting eight of them back to their mountain villages.

Soon all the prisoners had been released back to their families on the payment of 90 cents. Eventually only two remained, Feng and Sheng Li who had no families to buy them back. In the end Gladys was persuaded to pay for them which meant they stayed with her for a long time but proved to be very helpful. They trusted and respected Gladys. When she'd been quelling the riot in the prison, she never imagined she would end up buying two of them.

There was also the problem of Sualan, a pretty slave girl, who nobody claimed and also had nowhere to go. Gladys ended up taking Sualan along with her.

After this Gladys went back to the hills. She had grown to fear the Japanese with their barbaric ways and was bitterly opposed to the persecution of the Chinese. As she had assumed Chinese citizenship, she resolved to do something about it.

Romance had never featured strongly in Gladys' life. She had enjoyed the kind of romance that she had seen in films back in England, but nothing like that had ever happened to her. Her love for God was the driving force in her life, along with her love for her children. She was too busy to pay any special attention to her looks or her dress. All that changed one spring day while she was still living at the Inn.

'Do you care about China?'

The dignified speaker stood before her, his shiny dark hair brushed back from his high forehead. His dark, almond shaped eyes held her stare.

'Of course I care about China.'

'Do you believe the Japanese are an evil force trying to over-run China?'

'Yes, of course, they're an evil force.'

'Then will you help me?'

Gladys was in a difficult position. She had come out to China to preach the gospel, but surely God would have wanted her to oppose evil in every shape and form. In her own mind, Gladys debated the issue and eventually, she answered, 'I will help you as far as my conscience will allow.'

This compromise seemed to satisfy the young official who promised to return soon. Linnan was a member of the Intelligence Service of the Nationalists led by Generalissimo Ley. He had been educated in Peking and trained at the Central Military Academy of Nanking.

And so began a friendship between two intelligent people of similar ages, who were both trying to do what was right. They met whenever they could and debated, talked and laughed. Linnan showed a concern for Gladys that she had not experienced before, he really seemed to care about her safety. Gladys had had few close friends in the past, and a close mutual affection grew between them.

At one time during a period of fighting, her prayer book was recovered from the fields close to the city. Linnan feared she was dead and even organised for mass graves to be opened up to see if a foreigner had been buried among them. He was all the more relieved when they eventually met up again.

Gladys began to use her visits to the mountain villages to report to Linnan on the whereabouts of the Japanese army. When possible she was able to tell him about their numbers and armaments. It was dangerous work, but Gladys seemed to thrive on it. She tried not to think too hard whether she was doing this to please God or Linnan.

The attitude she took at this time was to cause great trouble for her friends later on. David Davies became concerned and tried to warn her of the dangers, but Gladys had always been headstrong and single minded. She had an almost childlike reasoning and she paid no attention to David's warnings. Japanese soldiers were often in her meetings, so she was betraying their trust as well.

It was a complex war. The Japanese were fighting the Chinese and the whole area of Shansi was a battlefield. Guerillas were in the mountains. Nationalist troops belonging to Chiang Kai-shek fought alongside troops belonging to the local war lords. Communist troops from Szechwan attacked both the Chinese Nationalists and the Japanese. David tried to keep his mission station neutral, but Gladys had no such intention.

It was to be David who paid the price of her indiscretions, not Gladys herself. About this time David had agreed to escort two elderly European ladies to Chifu on the coast, a month's journey away. Gladys was left in charge at Tsehchow as David had already sent Jean and the children away because he was concerned about the situation. He wished he had been able to send Gladys away as well.

Before he left both he and Gladys were injured by the Japanese who broke into the women's quarters during one night. When David heard the commotion he rushed in to find what was happening. He was appalled to find about thirty Japanese soldiers had broken in and were beginning to beat the women. Gladys had been knocked to the ground unconscious.

David knew he could do nothing against all these soldiers, so above the din, he shouted, 'Pray, pray.'

The women fell to their knees and started praying. One soldier pulled out his gun and held it to David's head. As he pulled the trigger nothing happened; it had jammed. He then hit David on the head with it and he collapsed to the ground. The women continued praying and the soldiers, not sure what was happening, retreated.

While David took Jean and the family to the coast, Gladys was left in charge. She was continuing her spying activities, although she didn't see them as such, because she was now Chinese. David was refused permission to return to Tschow, but he was so worried about conditions there, he returned secretly, using some lesser-known mule-tracks. It was a journey of a thousand miles and it took him a long time.

Gladys went on with her visits to the remote villages with her basket of supplies over her arm and periodically reported back to Linnan. She had a deep mistrust and dislike towards the Japanese because of the way they had treated some of her converts. It was an aversion that was to last all her life.

Many years later, the film *The Inn of the Sixth Happiness*, which portrayed her life, made much of her friendship with Linnan, and in true Hollywood style turned it into a romance. Gladys vehemently denied any such intimacy, and later said of the film, 'I never had a love scene like that in my life.'

It was while the Davies were away that Gladys had a visit from a young American press correspondent, Theodore White. He was staying with the Evangelical Alliance Mission of the USA. Searching for a good story, he found Gladys was only too willing to tell hers. She was a gift to any journalist and he was amazed at how frank she was. He, of course, encouraged her as it was not every day he met a real live spy. Gladys was naïve, or as she often described herself, 'silly'.

When White returned to the Scandinavian Alliance, as it was then known, he wrote an article for *Time Magazine* about his encounter with this little missionary. The information contained in his article was later used as evidence against David Davies when he stood before a tribunal of Japanese officers, accusing him of being a spy.

The situation in Shansi deteriorated into a living nightmare. Gladys moved from place to place, sometimes at the hospital cave at Bei Chai Chuang and sometimes in the town of Chin Shui. At one time nearly a hundred refugees were hiding in the small church in Ching Cheng with Japanese soldiers stationed out the front of the church and Nationals at the back.

After many days it was becoming like a siege as food was running out. Inside the church they prayed regularly and one morning, ten to twelve strong animals pulled into the churchyard dragging heavy carts of military supplies. The drivers hurriedly got out of the trucks and ran away. Gladys never discovered who had sent the trucks, but the supplies saved their lives of those in hiding.

On another occasion in another village, Timothy and Wan Yu, two of her young boys, saw Japanese soldiers at the end of the street. Gladys was worried about all the children hiding with her for if the Communist guerrillas found them, they would be recruited.

Suddenly one of the boys called,

'The soldiers are getting nearer. The Japanese are here.'

Gladys could see that they had entered the village at the far end of the street and were searching every house. Gladys could hear them as they moved nearer and nearer. She decided to go out to meet them knowing it would be certain death for her, but trusting that the distraction might give the children time to escape. She got as far as the gate and stood there with her hand on the latch, praying, when suddenly she heard Wan Yu call out, 'They're going away down the hill.'

Gladys knew another miracle had occurred. God had kept her safe once again and was caring for the children.

Gladys had no thought of escaping from the war-torn area. She regarded the Chinese as her people and she wanted to live and die with them.

'Chui tao tu pu twai' she said (Christians never retreat).

Events, however were to dictate otherwise. As Gladys moved from mountain village to mountain village more and more refugees gathered, including about two hundred children, mostly orphans. Everyone was becoming very worried about their safety. They heard that Madame Chiang Kai-Shek, wife of the head of the Chinese government was a Christian and had set up a home for war orphans in Sian.

It was decided to take the children to safety there. First, an evangelist, Tsin Pen Kuang would take a group of about one hundred children to Sian and then return for the others. David also hoped that he would be able to get rid of Gladys at the same time, both for her safety and his. He could not order her to leave, as she wasn't working for the China Inland Mission. He knew she was prepared to die, rather than change her ways. She didn't realise what a liability she was. What neither of them knew was that one of the greatest events was about to take place in Gladys' life, one would that would eventually make her known all over the world.

Tsin Pen Kuang went off with about a hundred children. After a hazardous journey, they all arrived safely. Gladys and David waited for him to return, but sadly he was killed on his way back. Not knowing this sad fact, they continued to wait for him.

David wanted Gladys to leave. Gladys wanted to stay, but eventually matters were decided for them.

Out in the street Gladys was met by a Nationalist soldier who handed her a piece of paper, saying that copies of it were posted all over the villages. She was stunned by what she read:

'One hundred dollars reward will be paid by the Japanese Army for information leading to the capture of "The Small Woman", know as "Ai-wei-deh".'

The trek commences

Gladys knew her life was in great danger. The Japanese would show her no mercy if she were caught, so she had to get away immediately, but how? The Japanese controlled all the main routes. The Chinese Nationalists were retreating. Pillaging and ravaging were taking place in every city, village and hamlet. Now that Gladys had a price on her head, she knew many people would betray her for a hundred dollars—which was a great deal of money to the Chinese.

She travelled to Tsechow to ask for help and advice from David, but she was still loathe to leave. She felt God had called her to Yangcheng. Her people were there and she was needed there. To leave was like running away. She turned to prayer, but at first could find no answer until her eyes fell on a passage she couldn't remember reading before.

'Flee ye, flee ye into the mountains, dwell deeply in hidden places, because the King of Babylon has conceived a purpose against you.'

The Japanese were indeed her King of Babylon. Gladys made plans to depart, while David realised that this was all part of God's plan. There was still much concern over the hundred children who were with Gladys; if they could all leave together, they might be saved. They knew the first children had arrived safely on the other side of the Yellow River, but they also knew that Tsin Pen Kuang had not returned. David and Gladys had been waiting for his return to send the rest of the children to a place of safety. Now it seemed as if Gladys would have to take them.

David was very worried. There was no suitable man to travel with Gladys, so what chance would she stand with all these children? The route was even more dangerous now, but there was no choice. They would simply have to trust that God would protect them.

In the spring of 1940 there were still plenty of children. Some came from the school in Tsechow, some were Gladys' own children and others came from families in and around Yangcheng, along with refugees who had joined them. They began to prepare for their long journey.

Gladys was sorry to leave David Davies behind as she had always been fond of the Davies. She felt that she was going into grave danger, but she later learned that it was David who fell into the danger, while she remained safe.

When Gladys had spoken so openly to the journalist, Theodore White, he had returned to America and published the information. Later he had written to Gladys thanking her for all her information she had told him about the movement of Japanese regiments. While Gladys was preparing to leave, she destroyed all her correspondence. Unfortunately, she had missed this one letter, which had somehow slipped down behind the desk. When the mission fell into Japanese hands, they gave the place a thorough search and found the incriminating letter. By now Gladys had departed, but David was still there. It was futile to tell the Japanese he knew nothing about Theodore White and that he had not even been at Tsechow when the journalist was there. The Japanese did not believe him or want to believe him. Although it was really Gladys they wanted, they intended to punish David instead.

The Japanese tried to make him admit, under torture that he was a spy. They starved him, and beat him, but he would not confess to something that was not true. His Christian companions were tortured and even put to death, but they didn't incriminate him. He said he knew nothing about a Mr White or the letter which was true; he had been a thousand miles away at the time.

After three months David was moved to a Chinese gaol at Tai Yuan. He was placed in a steel cage with other prisoners while an electric light glared down on them continuously. They had to kneel, stand or lie down to order.

Although the Japanese were trying to make him go insane, God was with him. David kept his sanity. For six months he was confined to this cell, until eventually he was moved to a better one.

After two years as a prisoner, he was taken to the coast and set free. While he was waiting for the last ship to take him home, he learned that his wife and children were in a camp nearby and he was able to join them. His small daughter, Ruth, who had never been very strong, had contracted whooping cough and just after the last ship sailed, Ruth, his only daughter, died.

For the rest of the war, Jean, David and their two small boys stayed in the internment camp. Eventually they returned to England and settled down.

David's physical scars remained, but spiritually he was healed. He did not blame Gladys for her indiscretions. He merely said, 'She did what she believed to be right.'

Back in China, the party was preparing to leave. There were nearly a hundred children to travel with Gladys. She had Ru Mai to help her and a few of the older boys and girls, but mostly they were quite young children and there was much preparation needed for such a difficult journey.

Each child was given a small bowl, chopsticks, a face towel and a little quilt for bedding. On their feet they had their straw sandals and many were able to carry a spare pair. But this was woefully inadequate for the journey ahead. Gladys had found it difficult obtaining even these small provisions. Never had an expedition been so ill equipped.

The local people were concerned about the conditions they would have to face and the magistrate agreed to send two of his local men to carry the food, staying with the party for a couple of days.

There was no time to lose but a short prayer for their safety was given before they left. It was a tearful farewell. Gladys looked longingly at the city as she left, knowing she would never see it again.

What a sight they looked. Each child, even the youngest, was clutching their few possessions. Gladys was at the front of the procession, followed by happy, skipping little children. The mountains echoed with the sound of their singing the English choruses that Gladys had taught them. Behind Gladys were the slightly older children who were aware that this wasn't just an afternoon stroll. Bringing up the rear were the two men with the supplies of food swinging from their carrying poles. As they climbed higher and higher, the city looked smaller and smaller in the distance. At a bend in the mountain track, Gladys looked back. She remembered her first sight of the city and how beautiful it had looked in the evening light. Today the ruins and scars of war all too were visible. Gladys turned her back on it all, drew herself to her full height and moved on.

As they set off up into the hills, Gladys thought about her group. Besides herself, Ru Mai was the only adult. Ninepence and Sualan were the oldest girls. Then there were about eighteen other girls between the ages of thirteen and fifteen. Seven boys were between eleven and fifteen, including Teh and Liang who were the most responsible. The rest of the small children were between four and eight years old.

Their destination was beyond the Yellow River, to Fufeng in Shensi. There they would go to Madame Chiang's orphanage, which would be suitable for the younger children. The older girls would be taken to an organisation called the Good News, which Gladys assumed, because of its name, was Christian.

The first night was a pleasant adventure. They were able to sleep in a Buddhist temple. Most of the monks were away so there was plenty of room for them to spread themselves out. The little ones enjoyed running in and out of the various rooms and were well fed and comfortable.

On the second night they had to sleep out under the stars. The younger children were becoming tired and wanted to go back to the comforts of Yangcheng.

On the third day the two local men had to return home and as there was now less food to carry, this could be done by the older boys.

By now they were all becoming weary and the little ones especially wanted to rest more. Some of them were clinging on to Gladys' hand or being carried by her. But they dared not delay. They needed to travel south to cross the Yellow River before the Japanese reached it and they had no way of knowing how close they were behind.

To encourage them, Gladys sang choruses with the children. She taught them new ones and they sang the old ones with her. She smiled as she heard the words echoing around the mountains. Never before would such sounds have been heard in such remote places.

After several days, the children's shoes began to wear out as they trudged along the stony paths. Some were able to put on a spare pair that they were carrying, but others Gladys had to keep together with old rags.

It was becoming more difficult to find places to sleep. One evening as night fell, they were fortunate enough to find a cave to shelter in, but their joy turned to horror in the morning when they found it was full of snakes. There were even more snakes than children! After that Gladys preferred to sleep in the open.

On the sixth day when they were even more tired, Gladys was encouraging them to keep going although she knew there was still a long way to go. Yuan and Teh were up ahead to ensure the way was safe when suddenly Teh called out, 'Ai-wai-deh. There are soldiers coming round the corner!'

No sooner had he shouted than the soldiers appeared. Gladys prepared to blow her whistle as a signal that the children should scatter. She hesitated. If the children scattered, they might become lost, but if they stayed, they would be captured.

As she hesitated, she realised that the soldiers were Chinese Nationalists.

These men, about fifty in number, were reinforcements from Honan going to join the Nationalist force further north. They couldn't believe their eyes when they saw hoards of children so far from civilisation. Gladys explained they were heading for the Yellow River in the hope of crossing it before the Japanese arrived.

Even as she spoke there was the familiar drone of planes overhead and everyone rushed into the sparse bushes. Fortunately the aircraft had another destination and continued on their way, appearing not to notice them. Children and soldiers emerged from the bushes, laughing together, and returned to the path.

The best thing about meeting the soldiers was that they had food and were willing to share it. Although it was only normal army rations, food had never tasted so good. Gladys and her large party ate till they could eat no more and there was still enough left over for the soldiers. Gladys didn't know when they would be able to eat again and although she enjoyed the food, by now she was suffering from a fever. She had neglected herself for the sake of the children, but now there could be no delay, danger was creeping up behind them.

The Yellow River

'It's just down there. The river at last.' One of the boys who was up ahead suddenly shouted and pointed. They all rushed to the brow of the hill to see. For about twelve days they had been walking towards this point. 'Are we safe?'

'Will we be able to get across?'

'Will they have food for us, I'm starving?'

Gladys looked at the silver ribbon in the distance and gave thanks to God. Once across the Yellow River they would be safe. There would be food, rest and shelter for them. Gladys knew she couldn't go on much further. They still had a few small hills to climb, but everyone felt better just for having seen the river. In sight was their destination, the village of Yuan Ku on the banks of the river.

Led by the older boys, who still had some strength left, they rushed towards the outskirts of the village but no-one ran to meet them and no people could be seen going about their daily business. In fact the village was completed deserted as the villagers, afraid of the arrival of the Japanese, had hidden themselves.

As Gladys looked towards the river, her face fell. There were no boats on the water to ferry them across. They were trapped with the river in front and the Japanese behind. Gladys sat down and cried. They had travelled so far, the journey had been so hazardous and now it looked as if they were beaten. The children joined in Gladys' disappointment.

Hwang Ho, the Chinese name for the river, meant China's Sorrow. It was a very appropriate name for a river responsible for the drowning of a million people. In 1852 when it was 2,600 miles long and a mile wide, it suddenly changed course. It now entered the sea some 250 miles further south than its original place, drowning thousands in its change.

At a later stage in the war, the Nationalists opened the dykes of this river in a vain attempt to stop the Japanese advance. Hundreds of miles of riverside hamlets and villages were swept away and very many people drowned. China's Sorrow indeed.

None of this went through Gladys's mind as she stood on its banks, viewing the deserted stretch of water with no boat in sight. Hunger and disappointment were her main feelings as she sat on a boulder looking at the weary children around her. The ache in her stomach was both physical and emotional.

The older boys were able to find a few scraps of mouldy food that had been left by the fleeing inhabitants, but only the younger children were fed. The rest were very hungry indeed as they went to sleep that night. Gladys was unable to sleep.

She was hungry, tired and suffering from a fever. In addition, the injuries she had received from the Japanese were troubling her now.

They stayed there for two days, waiting for something to happen. Gladys didn't know what to do next. There was no boat to take them across, and nobody to give them food. She was worried and frightened by her responsibilities and felt like giving up; God had let her down. In the midst of her misery, Sualan spoke to her;

'You know the story you told us about Moses taking the people of Israel across the Red Sea?'

'Yes.' Gladys replied cautiously, anticipating the conversation.

'If God did that for Moses, couldn't he get us across?'

Gladys was tired, hungry and ill and could sometimes be very sharp tongued when she was cross.

'Yes God did, but we are not living in those days and I'm not Moses.'

The reply came back quietly and full of trust;

'No, but God's still God.'

Gladys sat quite still. Her own faith had been almost non-existent, but now one of her girls had shamed her. Of course, God had protected them in the past. He wouldn't let them down now. He hadn't brought them here to die.

'Yes, Sualan. We'll pray. Everyone down on your knees.'

What a sight they must have made, all kneeling, down by the Yellow River. Afterwards they got up and continued trying to find scraps of food, while the younger ones splashed about at the water's edge.

Suddenly they heard the sound of soldiers approaching and there was nowhere to hide. Gladys sat quite still, praying. As the soldiers got nearer she saw they were wearing the uniform of the Chinese Nationalists and not the enemy. God had answered their prayers.

The soldiers couldn't believe what they were seeing. They had expected the area to be deserted and here were children playing in the water. A tall, young officer approached Gladys with a look of incredulity on his face.

'What are you doing here? Don't you know the Japanese will be here very soon?'

'Of course we know they will. That's why we need to cross the river. We're going to Sian.'

'It's forbidden for anyone to cross the river. The safest thing you can do is to return to the mountains.'

'We're not going back. I've got to get these children to safety.'

Gladys drew herself to her full height and glared up at him. He scratched his head. He had never encountered a problem like this before. Nor had he met such a determined woman. He wondered if he could force them to return to the mountains, but one look at Gladys' face convinced him that he would be wasting his time. Reluctantly, he blew his whistle.

Unnoticed by the group was a ferry on the opposite bank. At the summons of the whistle, it made its slow way towards them.

'Oh look,' cried one of the children, 'Isn't God wonderful. He knows we're too tired to walk any further, so he's sent us a boat.'

The soldier wasn't so spiritually minded.

'There are so many of you. It will take about three journeys to get you all across.'

'That doesn't matter so long as we get across.'

'Yes, but the Japanese will probably bomb when you're half way across and I don't want to lose any of my men.'

Carefully, they got onto the ferry. It was another adventure for the children, but it was a further worry for Gladys as she scanned the sky for enemy planes. However, after three trips they were all safely over and no Japanese planes had appeared. As a bonus, the soldiers had given the children some thin porridge, which sustained them for a short while.

On the other side of the river, they found the villages were still inhabited. Gladys was able to treat the sick and injured, bathing their feet and washing their sores. She was also able to replace some worn out shoes.

The children were very resilient. As conditions had slightly improved, they were full of high spirits again. It was the older ones and Gladys who still felt very fatigued. On and off, Gladys still suffered from a fever and seldom did she have enough to eat. She gave her food to the children whenever she could.

'What's that?'

'I'm frightened.'

'It's coming to eat us up.'

At the town of Mien Chih in Honan, the children encountered a train for the first time in their lives for there were no railways in the mountainous regions around Yangcheng. To continue their journey they had to get on this monster. As the black steam locomotive drew nearer, the younger children ran to hide. The elder ones stood as far back as they could. Peeping out from their hiding places, the young children saw that Gladys had not moved, nor had she been harmed, so sheepishly, they came back.

Refugees were allowed to travel on trains for free, which was just as well, because Gladys had no money. This meant the train was very crowded and the children had to squash into the compartments, or make themselves as comfortable as they could on the floor.

It was a journey of new experiences for the children. The first time the train was about to enter a tunnel, a man in the compartment proceeded to light a candle. Some of the boys, either thinking it was dangerous or simply for fun, blew it out. At that moment the train entered the tunnel and many of the children cried out in fear, until the man was able to light his candle again.

The train journey lasted four long days. Even Gladys was pleased to disembark and walk to the next village. Many people were kind to them on their journey, including a number of other refugees. Now they had crossed the Yellow River, they were not always happy with the food they were offered. They were used to eating maize, but the staple diet here was rice and their tender stomachs were not used to it. On one occasion they had to eat bread!

There was still another mountain range to traverse. Gladys, suffering ill health, felt she could go no further and the children were becoming increasingly tired and hungry. Nobody appreciated the beautiful scenery any longer, and Gladys knew she had to get the children to safety soon or they would perish on the mountainside.

Tung Kwan was the next village reached. Another train was needed for the following part of the journey to get to Hwa Chow, their next destination but there were no passenger trains running for fear of the enemy. Gladys was in despair and was finding it hard to pray at this time.

Eventually, someone remembered there was a coal train due to travel through the night to Hwa Chow. It would be a dangerous journey, as Japanese troops were stationed on the other side of the river which the train passed by and very often the train was shot at even at night. Nevertheless, there was no other alternative.

'They'll have to hide among the coal and not make a sound.'

'They certainly won't make a sound. They'll fall asleep in a moment.'

In fact, the younger ones were already asleep, so Gladys and the older boys were able to pick them up gently and lay them in the trucks. Then they wedged themselves in between the lumps of coal as the train started on its slow journey. All through the night it chugged along the side of the river towards the next town. Although the sounds of the Japanese could be heard across the river, no shots were fired. The younger ones slept through it all, but the older ones did not.

In the morning the younger children awoke with a shcok. Not only were they on a moving train, they were also black from head to foot. Astonished eyes peered out of blackened faces as they surveyed each other.

'Oh, look we're on a train again.'

'You've got a black face.'

'You're all black except your eyes and teeth.'

To the children it was a further adventure.

The next night was spent in a Chinese temple, which provided a place to sleep and something to eat. Excited, noisy children ran through the hallowed corridors. Nothing was sacred.

A weight fell off Gladys' shoulders as they approached the city of Sian. She had kept the children going with tales of their expected welcome and the fact that their journey would be over but as they approached the city walls, they could see that the gates were closed, no further person was allowed inside. The city of Sian was filled to overflowing with refugees.

Gladys had no choice, they had to continue. She had been going to take only the older girls to Fufeng; now everyone would have to go there. It meant two more days trekking and a train journey of five days. Gladys was now so weak, that some of the older boys had to help her, but she knew she must keep going, as the safety of the children depended on her.

The first hundred children to leave Yangcheng had been brought by Tsin Pen Kuang to Fufeng, but their journey had been so easy by comparison. There had been fewer refugees and more trains.

Gladys lost all count of time as they travelled. All she knew was it had been March when they commenced their journey and now it was April. They had passed through many different types of countryside, mountains and plains, but Gladys was too exhausted to appreciate the scenery and felt like her journey would never end.

In this year, 1940, Gladys knew nothing of the conditions on the other side of the world. She did not know that Britain was at war with Germany, that America and the Far East were being drawn in and that her own family were in danger from the bombs that were dropping on London. All she knew about was what was going on in her small part of China and that she had to succeed at all costs.

At last the day arrived when they reached the city of Fufeng. There was no special welcome and no reception party. They were just another small band of refugees, dirty and bedraggled but happy to have reached the safety of the city. It was a tearful parting having talked, eaten, laughed and endured dangers, hardships, hunger and exhaustion together and now they were to part. With some sadness but also great relief, Gladys handed her charges over into safe-keeping.

It was an anticlimax for her. What should she do now? Where should she go? Her first need was to find accommodation for herself. At Fufeng there was a little mission station where she was able to stay, but she felt disorientated. Having badly neglected the needs of her body, she had suffered such severe hunger that she was unable to keep down the food she was offered. She had reached her goal, but could not now unwind or relax. She did not know what she was supposed to do now and she felt very ill and tired.

There were no actual missionaries at the station, but the occupants made her welcome. They knew nothing about her, except that she had brought some children over the mountains from Yangcheng. It seemed she had a story to tell, so they asked her to speak at one of their meetings.

Before the meeting started, Gladys felt tired and asked if she could have a short rest. Two hours later she was found still lying on the bed, but by now delirious and raving. A doctor was sent for and it was later discovered she was suffering from a fever, pneumonia and dysentery. The brave, heroic Ai-weh-deh was seriously ill and it was expected she would die.

Recovery to Health

'**B**ut who is she?' 'Where has she come from?' 'Where was she going?' 'We don't know. We don't know anything about her.' 'What's wrong with her? We must get her to the American missionary in Hsing Ping. He'll know what to do. He might know who she is.'

Realising she was a westerner, two Chinese peasants placed this small, seriously ill woman on an ox-cart and took her to the only suitable place they knew, the American Mission. They didn't know who she was either, but they did know she was dangerously ill and likely to die. It was only by God's provision she hadn't collapsed during the journey, for what would have happened to all the children then? No one could have led them to safety. God in his providence, had allowed her to keep going until all the children were safe. At least, now she was in Hsing Ping, she could be taken care of.

The American missionary worked out that she was English, although she was jabbering away in a mixture of Chinese dialect and English. He could not make much sense of what she was saying. She talked about Yang and Violet, she rambled on about bombs and British film stars. In desperation he wired the Baptist Missionary Society,

'Unknown British woman seriously ill doctor please come. Gustafsen.'

Dr Handley Stockley and a nurse, Miss Francis Major, travelled over. As they didn't know what was wrong with her they brought plenty of medical equipment with them, blood film slides, medicines, needles, syringes, distilled water and intravenous saline of glucose. They soon discovered Gladys had a temperature of 105°F and was suffering from fatigue and malnutrition. The nurse managed to administer a sedative.

Dr Stockley treated her for a short while, but then had to return to his own mission station. Five days later he was called back. Her temperature had again risen to 105° and she was discovered, through tests, to have contracted typhus, pneumonia, typhoid fever and relapsing fever. She was also suffering from the beating she received many months earlier.

Gustafsen told Dr Stockley that he had just been given a new drug from America—sulphapyridine sulphur 693; would it save this patient? God had gone before. This drug was the only one capable of pulling Gladys back from the brink of death. Along with loving care of those at the Mission, it saved her life. However, the next problem was what to do with her as she slowly regained her health.

She was taken to Sian, but reacted very badly to the noise of the bombing on that city. It was imperative to move her to somewhere more peaceful.

God's help came through a dog. Missionaries were expected to deal with every eventuality and one day, a local man brought his dog into the compound with a thorn in its paw. Gustafsen knew that the dog's owner lived at the Great Goose Pagoda just outside the city and thought this could be an ideal place for Gladys to recuperate.

Later, Gladys could remember very little about this period. She did as she was told, she went where she was sent, but seemed to have no will of her own. As her recovery progressed, it was decided she should stay with Hubert and Mary Fisher, Baptist Missionaries, who lived at Meihsien.

Gladys was still very ill. She suffered from hallucinations and sometimes became deranged. Her confused mind still went back to various events in her past. One moment she was raving about the mountain trek, the next she was talking with her Mum and sister Vi and then she was convinced she was back at Yangcheng with Jeannie.

It was at Meihsien that Gladys reached her lowest point spiritually. She felt so near to death. In 1940, at Meihsien she wrote in her diary, despairingly and with determination, 'I shall not die'.

She also recorded the help she received from the text in 2 Chronicles 32:7, which she paraphrased as: 'Be strong and of a good courage. Do not be afraid and do not wobble. Is not your God with you?' Meihsien, June 1940

For six months Gladys stayed with Hubert and Mary Fisher while her physical strength gradually returned. They had first met Gladys a few years earlier in the western mountains of Shansi and remembered on that occasion, Gladys had called a very early prayer meeting, to pray for funds as her own had been given away to needy people.

At first Gladys could not keep any food down as she was suffering from dysentery, but slowly her health improved helped by Mary's excellent cooking. At a later stage her health deteriorated again when she was away from Mary's care. Besides the good food, Gladys appreciated the opportunity to converse in English.

After six months, Gladys improved sufficiently to be able to move back to Fufeng with Ru Mai into a three-room house with a dirt floor, and in true Chinese style, a k'ang to sleep on. At this time she did not take care about her eating habits, and became very tired again.

While she was here, Gladys also received information about the Good News organisation. With her usual simple trust, she had thought this was a Christian organisation because of its name. She now found out that it arranged to send young girls to the north-west of China to become wives and servants in an area that was short of young, strong females.

Regaining some of her former strength of character, Gladys marched up to the establishment, demanded to take the girls away and took them back with her. In actual fact she'd broken the law, for she had willingly left the girls in their care. Miraculously, she was not restrained or reported.

Money again became a problem. Gladys was able to earn a small amount of money by giving English lessons to officials who wanted to learn the language. Again, Gladys recalled with amusement how she had been turned down by a missionary society as too old to learn Chinese yet was now using that language to teach English.

Gladys had become so involved in the war in China that she didn't know what was going on in the rest of the world. It was difficult for any post from England to reach her, so she completely lost touch with her family and with world affairs. In 1941 she wrote to her parents,

'It's 1941 and I've only just heard you've got your own war in Europe.'

She felt guilty that she was not able to support her family in their struggles, but when she looked back on what she had suffered, she knew she could identify with them. While the wars in China were going on, it was difficult for her to get her letters out and she would not know until months later whether her news had reached England or not.

As the years moved on her Chinese family was growing up and the older ones were moving on. Before long, Ninepence was married, using the small dowry that had been left to her. She then moved away and had a little boy of her own. The second member of Gladys' family, Less, became a Nationalist soldier and was later shot by the Communists which gave Gladys a further reason for her aversion to that regime.

The Baptist missionaries nearby were worried about Gladys. It was becoming increasingly unsafe for her to remain in the country, but there was nowhere else they could send her and in any case she would not go anywhere. All she wanted to do was to return to Yancheng and continue her work there.

What she did not know was that, when Jean and the children had been sent to the coast, David himself had been captured by the Communists and was to remain in their clutches for many years.

Later, Gladys rented a room in Sian to which other refugees could come. With the war still in progress, there were many people looking for accommodation and divided families and lost souls were all made welcome with Gladys for she knew what it was to be a refugee herself and she was able to tell them about a much earlier refugee, Jesus.

Dr Stanley Hoyte

The missionaries were still not sure what to do with Gladys. She was a law unto herself and found it difficult to work as a member of a team. Her attitude was 'Me and God'. She acted as if she had a straight line to God and had little regard for the opinions of others.

At one period she stayed with Dr and Mrs Hoyte in Lanchow in the north east on the banks of the Yellow River, at Seaside, Temple Hill, Chefoo which was a school for missionary children and had been the compound of a leprosy hospital. Gladys found Lanchow a busy place as it was a route for travellers going to Central Asia. She only stayed a fortnight before her restless spirit made her want to move on. This was becoming a very unsettling time for her.

Grace Hoyte

Travelling south to Tsinsui, snows of the hard winter had closed the mountain passes, and Gladys remained in a remote Muslim mountain village for the whole season. She felt very lonely and ill at ease there and was still suffereing recurring bouts of illness and the spirit worship in the village made her feel oppressed.

She also spent some time in the neighbouring CIM mission station, but did not stay for long. She felt she wanted to go to Szechwan but had no money to get there. She eventually travelled hundreds of miles south on a ramshackle bus to Chengtu and remained there for the last four years of her time in China.

When she became ill again, she was looked after by Dr Luke and Ruth Hsido for whom she then came to live and work. While she was staying there, the city of Chengtu experienced a religious revival and an Independent Christian Church was formed consisting of the three churches in the region, with Sam Jeffrey in charge of the mission station.

While in Chengtu, Jarvis Tien, a twenty-two year old refugee student stayed with Gladys. He became a Christian and was one of the few people who was able to help Gladys when she had one of her temporary periods of mental instability. He later went to America, did very well and occasionally sent her money.

Christian Chang, a new convert, became principal of the Theological Seminary in Nanking and was appointed pastor of the Methodist Church in Chengtu. He gave Gladys the job of Bible woman. This meant she could visit the women of the city in their homes and talk to them about the Bible. It was a wonderful opportunity to witness and she was probably the only westerner to be appointed to that role.

Chaing Sao was another Bible Woman, who worked alongside Gladys. She had had a terrifying experience and miraculous escape when captured by the Communists of the 4th Route Army. Her friends were afraid she would be tortured into betraying secrets, but after only three days she returned, with a remarkable story to tell.

She had been taken to an unknown place and questioned. As her interrogator was from a different province they were unable to understand each other.

Despairing of making Chaing Sao understand his questions, the interrogator lost his temper. Chaing Sao was so terrified, that she just kept saying 'Jesus, Jesus.' As he still couldn't understand what she was saying, he became even crosser, but she kept repeating 'Jesus, Jesus Christ' again and again.

Chapter 16

On the third morning, all the prisoners were taken out of their cells and lined up with their faces towards a wall. Many fell down crying and screaming because of the beatings and kickings they were receiving. Chaing Sao feeling paralysed and weak in her legs and heard a voice say 'Chaing Sao, lean on me. Lean against my shoulder.' As she leaned on the unseen stranger for hour upon hour, she felt a great pain in her cheek and eventually a Communist soldier came up to her and said,

'Get out of here, you insane woman. Only an insane woman could have stood here for five hours without collapsing. Get out.'

As she staggered away she looked around her. Everyone else was dead, lying in their own blood. God had granted her a miraculous escape that day.

The job of Bible Woman provided Gladys a small allowance, so she was able to buy her daily food. Her other tasks included cleaning the church and visiting the leprosarium run by the West China Union University. Morale was very low among these badly deformed men who felt they had nothing to live for. However, Gladys was able to preach to them and some started coming to the church.

Gladys was still in touch with many of her children who had endured the epic journey with her. She made herself available when they needed help and a good number of them visited her.

Chu En was the son of a pastor who had been killed by the Japanese. His mother had died on the banks of the river at Yangcheng while trying to escape with her five young children, of which he was now the sole survivor. One sister had died of tuberculosis, another two were killed in raids while his younger brother had joined the 'Children's Army' and was slaughtered by the enemy.

Gladys was worried that she would not be able to afford to send him to school, as he seemed quite bright, but a Dr Tsung was willing to take him and educate him. This meant Gladys only saw him occasionally, but she was proud of the way this serious young boy was developing.

On one of his visits to Gladys, Chu En made a startling announcement.

'I'm going back to Yangcheng.'

Gladys was very worried.

'But you can't go back. All that's in the past now. Yangcheng is completely under enemy control now. There is no safety there.'

Then Chu En gave an argument she was unable to refute.

'When God called you to China, did you have to obey?'

'Of course.'

'Well, God has called me back to Yangcheng and I must go.'

Gladys knew Chu En must obey God and started to pray for his immediate needs. He desperately needed shoes and a pair of trousers but she received no answer to her prayers.

'It's because you're praying for the wrong things.' Chu En informed her.

'But you need shoes and a pair of trousers.' Gladys retorted.

'I came from Yangcheng without any shoes and these trousers will last a little longer. What I need is a stethoscope.'

'Why a stethoscope?' Gladys asked.

'I don't know, but God does.'

With that Gladys had to be content, but she didn't feel God would ever be able to answer that particular prayer.

A few days later an old refugee woman invited Gladys to her house. While she was there, Gladys noticed an unusual box in the corner. When she asked what it was, she was told it had been left behind by someone who had told her about Jesus.

Gladys looked in the box. She could hardly contain her amazement when she found inside, a thermometer, tweezers, scissors and right at the bottom, a stethoscope. The refugee had no use for these items and was pleased to let Gladys have them.

Chu En had always been confident God would answer his prayers and set off for Yangcheng as soon as he could. It was many months later Gladys had news of a young man going round the villages with a strange-looking instrument which he was placing on their chests, saying, 'We can see the outside of your body, but God can see the inside.'

There were many converts and baptisms in the area where Chu En was faithfully following God's plan for his life.

Revivals and persecution

While Gladys and her fellow Christians were praying for various parts of China, she was convinced that she should visit a particular unknown territory. A friend of hers, Dr Huang agreed to accompany her.

Together they ventured into this region, preaching the gospel wherever they could. One evening as night was falling, they stopped to pray for guidance as they had nowhere to spend the night.

'Dear God, please give us food and a place to sleep for the night,' prayed Gladys. Then as she listened to Dr Huang's prayer, she felt ashamed at her selfishness.

'Oh, God, we have been unable to witness to anyone today. Please send us someone we can tell of your love.'

To keep their spirits up, they started to sing. As their voices echoed round the mountainside, they heard the scrunch of stones as a Tibetan lama priest came hurrying towards them.

'Come, come, we are all ready for you.' The priest had picked up their bundles and was beckoning them to follow.

This was obviously the answer to Dr Huang's prayer, but they were still hesitant about following this man.

'Come along,' the Tibetan said, 'we are waiting for you to tell us about the gospel of love.'

Sure now that this was God's leading, they followed him to a monastery.

Once inside, they were treated almost reverently, given food and shown to their rooms. Gladys thought they could then settle down for the night, but she was wrong. They were summonsed to a large hall where about five hundred lamas were sitting cross-legged, waiting for their visitors to talk.

As Dr Huang told of God's love and sacrifice, Gladys almost felt she was in a dream situation. A woman was never allowed in the presence of lamas, but how wonderful was her God who had sent them on this mission.

The story of the priests went back many years. Some of them had been selling herbs in the local village when they heard a man shouting,

'Who wants salvation free and nothing to pay?'

They took the piece of paper, which was being offered and passed it round when they returned to the monastery. This piece of paper was shown to Gladys and Dr Huang.

'For God so loved the world that He gave His only begotten Son, that whosoever believeth on Him should not perish, but have everlasting life.'

The lamas were then able to go to a neighbouring village to a China Inland Mission where they were presented with a copy of the Gospels, Matthew, Mark, Luke and John. This they were able to study for the next few years, but were particularly struck by the words,

'Go ye into all the world and preach the gospel.'

By this they knew that someone would tell them more about this wonderful God. When they had heard Gladys and Dr Huang singing on the mountainside, they knew that the messengers had arrived. Only people who knew this wonderful God would be able to sing in such circumstances.

All night in twos, the lamas visited Dr Huang and Gladys in their rooms. Altogether they stayed at the monastery for ten days, as the lamas were anxious to learn all they could. Gladys was humbled again as she realised God had gone before.

Later on, she found herself working among prisoners again, as the second largest prison in China was situated in the next town to where she was staying. Feeling that God was urging her to speak to the prisoners, she applied for a pass.

'The prisoners in here are hardened criminals,' she was told by the governor, 'I have made no impression on them during the five years I have been here. You won't be able to do anything.'

'No, but my God can.' Gladys replied calmly. She got her pass.

Gladys was so short that a small mound was built for her to stand on as she spoke to the inmates as they went about their daily tasks. It was a hard time for her, but she was encouraged by the support of the lepers in the colony who were remembering her in prayer.

Very slowly and one by one, the prisoners were converted and would then start praying for their fellow inmates. The behaviour of the Christian converts was radically different from their former state.

One day four prisoners were brought into the prison chained together.

They were thrown roughly to the ground by their guards who stood over them with guns.

Prompted by God, Gladys asked if she could talk to them. Permission was refused and she was taken out by the gateman, but the souls of these men were on her conscience and she continued to pray for them.

Gladys then learned that three of them had died, but the fourth, Mr Shan, was still very much alive and causing as much trouble as he could. When Gladys approached to speak to him, she felt he was completely evil and took a strong dislike to him. When she spoke to him, he cursed her strongly and spat in her face. She began to feel a hatred for him and begged those in the leper colony to pray for her over her feelings.

On one occasion when the men were returning to their cells, forbidden to speak or for anyone to speak to them, an inner voice urged Gladys;

'Speak to Mr Shan.'

Internally, she argued,

'I can't, he hates me.'

But God persisted in his promptings, so eventually Gladys approached the man and placed her hand on his shoulder. She blurted out the first words that came into her mind.

'Mr Shan, aren't you very miserable?'

He threw off her hand with a curse. Afterwards, Gladys was appalled by what she had done, for in Chinese culture, no woman ever touches a man in public. She had a most miserable night reflecting on the incident, but later heard what had been the outcome.

Mr Shan was completely stunned by what had happened. As he sat on a stone in a daze, Dhu Cor, one of the first converts approached him.

'What's wrong?' Dhu Cor asked

'Did you see what happened? She touched me. She touched me as if she loved me.'

'Maybe she does love you.' Dhu Cor replied.

'But how can she love me. I'm a murderer and all I've ever done to her is curse and spit at her.'

'She loves you,' Dhu Cor explained, 'because she loves the God who sent his Son to die for you. Her God loves you.'

Through that simple act of Gladys, Mr Shan was converted and the revival that had been long awaited in the prison, finally began, but it had taken the intense dislike of Gladys for one prisoner to be broken, before such revival could begin.

In addition to working in the leper colony and the prison, Gladys applied to the local Methodist church to work as an evangelist. She began under the conviction from God, that she should clean up a large church, which had become neglected. Gladys felt that God wanted the hall prepared for a great work for him. Gladys felt she was being useful again, a feeling that was very necessary to her. With the help of others the hall was made ready in forty days.

Special meetings were held to which many people attended, including students from the nearby University. Many were saved, especially from among the students. Of the five hundred young people at the college, about two hundred gave their lives to God. They were to pay a high price for their faith, for by this time the war was over and the Communists were in power. Gladys came to dislike these men more than the Japanese as they were very opposed to Christianity.

The Communists made all the University students complete a questionnaire. Except for the last one, all the questions were very innocent but the final question asked whether they were for or against the Communist Party. Even knowing the power of the Communist regime, two hundred students declared that they were Christians and against the Party. They realised that by doing this, they would suffer loss of education, failure to obtain a job and physical persecution.

Those outside the college were unable to contact them but prayed. Meanwhile the two hundred were subjected to ridicule, their meetings were broken up, they were jeered at and indoctrinated. They refused to renounce their faith.

Finally, they were all rounded up in the town square, given one last chance to recant and then beheaded. Gladys never forgot the scene of mangled bodies lying scattered on the stones which were awash with their blood. The blood of martyrs, however is the seed of the church.

Leaving China

D r Olin and Esther Stockwell also worked at the mission, and one day Gordon, a young Christian appeared having been badly burned on his face and hands by a pressure lamp. Gladys looked after him while his health improved and later on Gordon was able to look after Gladys when she needed help.

After a while Gladys found further opportunities for evangelistic work, visiting the small churches between Chengtu and Chungking. Her strength was now fully recovered and these visits to the villages and talking to the women there were among the happiest times of her period in China.

She was not to remain in peace for long however. Missionaries were not welcome in China now and there was still a price on her head. Where could she go? What could she do?

Dr Stockwell decided to write to the Orphaned Missions Committee, an organisation for German missionaries, asking for help to get Gladys back to England. Although Gladys was neither an orphan nor a German, surprisingly they agreed to pay her boat fare from Shanghai to England. The CIM were also willing to provide a room for her at their headquarters in Shanghai and Dr Stockwell had a small fund for evangelistic work and decided to use it to pay her air passages from Chengtu to Shanghai. Plans were coming together for her return to England.

It was many years later, before Gladys found out what eventually happened to Dr Stockwell. He was captured by the Communists and imprisoned in China for two years from November 1950 to November 1952.

There was another problem to resolve. Gladys had no passport because it had been lost with all her other belongings in her flight from Yangcheng. It was necessary for her to go all the way to Nanking to obtain another one. This caused further delay, but by this time Gladys was anxious to go home herself. She had not seen her family for nearly twenty years, and wanted to get back to see them all again.

Yet another complication arose. The Communists were actively seeking Gladys since finding the letter from America which suggested she was a spy.

Fortunately, she got away in time, unlike David Davies who had paid the price.

At last everything was ready for Gladys to leave. She felt sad for she knew her heart would always be in China. She didn't know when, if ever, she would be able to return. As she departed, she took one last look at the mountains she loved and bade a sad farewell to her many friends.

Gladys reached Shangai without any further adventures, but before she was due to leave the city, she was prompted by God to go into the Shangai Bank. She had no idea why, but she felt she had to meet a man there. When she entered the bank, a bizarre conversation took place.

'Can I help you?' she was asked.

'Yes, I've come to meet a man.'

'Yes, madam, which man is that?'

'I don't know, but I'll know when I meet him.'

Much perplexed, the cashier suggested she sat down and wait.

No sooner had she sat down than an office door opened and out walked one of her children! It transpired that he had been working there for a while. It was a happy reunion, with much to talk about and he was also able to help by giving her money for the journey home. Again, God had gone before.

The local young people decided to do all they could to help Gladys get home. They sold some of their clothes and books to obtain money for her, indeed some even sold their shoes, so that when the time came for Gladys to leave, only two of the young people, those who still had their shoes, could accompany her to the airport.

Gladys smiled when she remembered how back in England before she ever left for China, she had bought two left shoes cheaply and travelled right across the world wearing them. Then she thought of the many years in China spent unbinding the feet of the little children and now again by selling their shoes, the students had raised money for her. There were many sermons in those thoughts.

There was also a problem of Gladys not possessing the necessary passes, but amazing things happened on her journey home. Officials checking the passes started to move towards her, but just before they reached her they turned back and she was not asked to produce any documentation.

A little further on the journey, Gladys saw two officials trying to communicate with each other. Their only common language was English, which they were finding very difficult. Gladys moved in to help, knowing Chinese as well as English, and helped them to order a cup of tea. The outcome was that they invited her to join them. This meant they spent time talking with her, instead of checking her pass!

At the port, the Northern Chinese official asked for her passport, but then got into conversation with her about the city of Peking. Suddenly Gladys had to move on and there was no time to sign her passport. None of these incidents were planned by Gladys, but as she later said, she got from the west of China to the east with only God for help.

It was on 1 October 1949 that General Mao Tse-Tung officially proclaimed the People's Republic of China. His regime persecuted the Christians, tortured missionaries and banned and burned the Bibles. Although by then Gladys had left China, she came to fear the Communists more than the Japanese. The Japanese had not initiated such widespread persecution.

Her return journey to England was much quicker than her outward trek and far less eventful. Although it took a few weeks, the journey on a Greek ocean liner was a comfortable one. She had time to reflect and wonder where all the years had gone. Nearly twenty years in China—some of which had been happy years but there had been sad years as well. She had made many friends and lost others. She had faced grave danger and even death but never once did she regret the fact that God had sent her to China.

Dressed in her Chinese clothes, she felt lost when she arrived in England. She had written to say she was returning, but when she arrived at the station, it seemed there was no one to meet her. She stood alone, in her pale green and silver patterned Chinese dress, marvelling at how England had changed in such a short time. In fact her parents and sister were there waiting for her, but they had not recognised this little Chinese woman as their 'Glad', and she did not recognise them either at first for they looked so much older. When they eventually found each other, it was an emotional reunion.

England

G ladys found England had changed a great deal since she had left for China all those years ago. The green fields of Edmonton had been replaced by rows and rows of houses, the roads were full of fast-moving traffic and the pace of life was much faster. People had less time to greet their neighbour or help those in need. Gladys realised sadly that when she had left, England had been a Christian country, now it was much less so.

At first, Gladys' sister had been pleased to keep the home running while her mother was out speaking at meetings. But in Gladys' absence, she had met and married Bert Braithwaite in the summer of 1945. It was one of the various family events that Gladys had missed and although she was pleased her family had increased, Gladys knew it was getting more and more unlikely that she herself would ever marry.

Rosina Aylward

While Gladys had been so active in China, her mother had not been idle. Although she had worried a great deal about Gladys, she was very proud of her. Rosina had always been a speaker at ladies' meetings and now she had something special to talk about. Any news of Gladys was relayed to each meeting and any letter from her was always read out in full.

Rosina had missed Gladys greatly, but passing on her news made her seem nearer. She made a habit of contacting the local newspapers, who were delighted to receive information of an Edmonton daughter serving God on the other side of the world.

So when Gladys did return to England, she was already well known. The people of Edmonton had heard stories of her adventures, and knew of her brushes with death and how God had provided miracles. They felt Gladys' friends in China were their friends. Church after church had heard the same talk from Rosina, as in each church she gave the same talk: 'Our Glad in China.'

People now knew what Gladys had been doing and the dangers she had faced and instead of preaching to the Chinese at the Inn of the Eight Happinesses or to the mothers, whose children's feet she was unbinding, or to prisoners, she was now speaking to her own people. The congregations were thrilled to hear of her experiences first-hand.

Like her mother, Gladys was a born speaker. In hypnotic tones she would recount some incident that had taken place in the distant land. Such was her power that her listeners could feel themselves in the Chinese city of Yangcheng or out on the barren mountains pursued by the Japanese.

Story after story would be told with her audiences sitting on the edge of their seats. Gladys told how when she was in her gravest danger, she felt she was surrounded by a ring of prayer. It was of course the prayers of those very people back at home which were protecting her.

Just as her audiences were deeply involved and comfortably listening to what she was saying, Gladys would suddenly thrust the knife in.

'What about you, my friend. Is God calling you to go? Is he calling you to the mission field? Will you hear his call? Will you go?'

The stage boards of the West End had lost a great talent when Gladys answered God's call to China. She could move an audience to tears, to laughter and then to tears again. As she had captivated the muleteers in the courtyard of the Inn, so she enthralled the Western audiences as they listened in ever growing numbers.

At first she only spoke locally. Worshippers at Tanners End Free Church or Edmonton Central Hall became used to seeing this tiny lady in her Chinese silken gown, accompanied by her proud parents or sister.

Many Christian papers were eager to interview her and hear accounts of her exploits. It wasn't every day they had a missionary with such exciting stories to tell.

Gradually, her fame spread. She became known all over the country. For seven years people flocked to hear this tiny woman, who at the beginning had been one of them and was now more Chinese than English.

Gladys was now being known outside the region of London. There were calls for her to speak all over the country. Yeovil, Weston-super-Mere, the Midlands; she even preached in Enniskillen in Ireland. She was labelled 'the parlour-maid, who became a missionary'. It gave ordinary people the thought that they too could be used by God.

It wasn't only church congregations who heard her. Hugh Redwood, a journalist of that time had written a book *God in the Slums*. He heard about this dynamic missionary and thought that her story should feature in one of the national newspapers. Redwood passed on some of the information to the night editor of one of the London Daily Newspapers.

Alan Burgess, another journalist, picked up on the information he read. He felt that this small woman, dressed in her Chinese dresses might be a suitable subject for one episode of his radio programme, *The Undefeated*. He arranged to interview her.

When he knocked on the door of 67 Cheddington Road, he was unimpressed by the diminutive figure that greeted him. He was doubtful whether she was a suitable subject for his series after all, which was supposed to be exciting and adventurous. Her drab high-necked Chinese dress obviously wasn't her best, while her hair was drawn back into two plaits tied round her head. The face was lined from the hardship of her life in the Far East. Her brown eyes behind her heavy horn rimmed glasses, regarded him seriously.

'Did anything interesting happen to you all those years you were in China.'

'No, it wasn't interesting, just hard work. No one would want to know about anything I've done.'

Gladys was not being falsely modest. She really didn't think anyone would be interested. Alan was beginning to agree, there did not seem to be any story of note here, but being the professional he was, he pressed her for more information.

'I did take some children over the mountains.'

'Over the mountains! How many children?'

'Nearly a hundred.'

'Nearly a hundred! How old were they?'

'Most of them were between four and eight.'

'Four and eight!'

'Yes, but seven of the boys were between eleven and fifteen and some of the girls were older. Then there was Ru Mai and myself.

'Ru Mai?'

Alan realised that in his amazement, he was just echoing Gladys' words. How mistaken he'd been, there was definitely a story here. He knew he had struck gold. Here was a story that he could not wait to tell. As he questioned her further, more and more facts emerged.

'Then there was the time I quelled a riot in the prison. Me and God, of course. I was so frightened when the man approached me with an axe.'

'Quelled a riot in a prison?'

'Then I bought Ninepence, for ninepence, of course. It was all the money I had.'

Now that Gladys had started to talk, all the memories came flooding back. She wanted to explain about China to this journalist, and make him realise how wonderful her God was. She felt no pride in herself. It was God who had been leading her and it was to God she gave all the praise.

Alan Burgess knew he was in the presence of someone quite remarkable. It was rare for a journalist to have such a scoop for a story. He interviewed her nearly every day for the next four months, until Gladys longed for the obscurity of China.

Alan was mainly responsible for the BBC series in which true stories of personal courage were dramatised and on the 11 October 1949, he was able to transmit a half hour radio programme entitled *Gladys Aylward, One of the Undefeated,* with Celia Johnson playing the part of Gladys. At the same time the BBC published a booklet on the series, of which fifteen pages, including pictures, were devoted to Gladys.

Gladys made many friends as she travelled round the country and people were kind to her and allowed her to stay with them for an indefinite period—as she did with Mrs Rosemary Brisco. While staying with Rosemary, Gladys was able to give hospitality to many Chinese immigrants who were finding England a strange country.

Wherever she stayed, she left little gifts for her hosts, often carefully hidden, so it took them a while to find them. This was fine, unless it was food. Gladys still had a sense of fun.

But like Jesus before her, it was the ordinary people to whom she felt particularly drawn. These people came to hear her in their thousands and years afterwards they all remembered vividly her minute figure and the great power that radiated from her. Many who heard her felt their lives had been enriched by the experience. Many felt led to dedicate more of their lives to God.

In the 1949–50 period when she was staying in the city, she regularly visited the London Bible College and on Tuesday afternoons, held a regular prayer meeting in the house where she was staying. One of those present remembered how they all simply prayed together in this very cold house, kneeling on the stone kitchen floor. There was never time for tea or sociability.

Gladys still found time for individuals. People were never simply crowds or masses. Dozens of tapes still exist of talks that she gave, so that subsequent generations can still hear the power of her message. She often gave direct messages to her listeners. 'God is calling you. Listen to what he has to say.'

Gladys helped to establish a hostel in Liverpool for the resident Chinese and visiting Chinese seamen. By the end of the Second World War, six thousand Chinese lived in Liverpool's Chinatown. In the war, Liverpool had been badly bombed and many Chinese lost their lives. More Chinese subsequently came to England to escape from Communism. Gladys knew how lonely they were.

Esme, a young welfare carer felt the call to work with the Chinese, but did not quite know what to do about it. At the end of 1956 she read a prayer letter from Gladys appealing for helpers in Liverpool. In February 1957, Gladys arranged to meet Esme in Liverpool as she had been praying for someone to help in the work in that city and Esme had been praying to know God's will for her. God answered both prayers. Esme was able to care for the children of the Chinese families while their parents went to work and was able to help the families generally. It was a help that would continue into the next millennium, long past Gladys' own death.

Gladys often had news of her children back in China. Many were refugees again. They needed money and clothes. In England, Gladys arranged jumble sales and other fund-raising events. She heard of mass executions taking place in China and she feared for them. She worried about Ninepence who was still in China, married with a child which made Gladys a grandmother. Michael, another of her children was now in Hong Kong, so at least he was safe from the Communist regime.

Her heart was still in China and Gladys wished her body was there too. Gladys was unhappy at the way England was turning into a materialistic country. In the period after the war, people had become very self-centred. She longed for China, but as it was now a Communist state it was not possible for her to return there.

Gladys had agreed to stay in England while her parents were alive, having to report at regular intervals to a police station because she was in fact an alien. In the case of her father, the re-union was not for long. In the winter of 1949, the man who had told her all she could do was talk, died. Thomas, her father was no longer with them. In 1955, Rosina, her mother, who had been such a support to her, also died. That only left Vi and Bert as her immediate family as Lawrence had moved further north and had sadly lost contact with the family. Gladys was now free to return to the Far East, but where could she go?

The Methodist Recorder, April 1963

Return to the Far East and publicity

On the 15 April 1957, Gladys Aylward set sail from Tilbury on the liner Cushan. As the Suez Canel was still closed, it was a long tedious journey via the Canary Islands, Cape Town and Singapore. In her impatience, she felt she would never get there.

With the People's Republic of China now closed to her. After a great deal of prayer and soul-searching she resolved to do the next best thing and stay in Hong Kong.

Gladys found this small province a complete contrast to the vast country of China. Just under four hundred square miles, three million people were crowded onto its land with sixty thousand of those living on boats. More than 90% of the inhabitants were Chinese, so Gladys felt at home to some degree.

Gladys in April 1963

The weather was vastly different from that of Yangcheng. Three quarters of the annual rainfall fell between May and September and Gladys arrived during this unpleasant rainy season. In spite of the heavy rainfall, the province was short of water so it was rationed to two hours in the morning and the same in the evening.

Many plans for new reservoirs and extra roads were under way, but the imported labour force, along with refugees from the Communist regime in China, all served to make the place more crowded. The temperature was a hot and humid 82°F, and to add to her discomfort, rice was the staple diet, as opposed to the maize she was used to in the north.

When she arrived, Gladys found plenty of work to do. She was delighted to meet up with many of her children and was heartbroken to hear of the deaths of others.

One day, while walking down a crowded, dusty road, she met one of her sons, Michael. Like her, he was concerned about the plight of the number of child refugees. Gladys felt it was providential that they had met and after much prayer, they set up the Hope Mission in the resettlement area of Kowloon. This became a mission that was able to help the wave upon wave of refugees. Gladys and Michael were even more pleased to find three godly men who could direct the work. Gladys felt that after her long spell back in England, she was at last doing something to help those in need.

Before long, Gladys felt it was not right for her to stay in Hong Kong any longer, so after only a few months, she sailed for Taiwan, also known as China's 23rd province. This beautiful island was still a free country. Only one hundred and twenty miles off the South East coast of Red China, and one hour's plane ride from Hong Kong, this island was then known to Gladys as Formosa. It was also known as China Free State, as it had not been overrun by Communism. Gladys fell in love with the place and when she was to have a new passport issued, stated Formosa, the earlier name for Taiwan, as her place of residence. She was home.

Back in England in 1957, Alan Burgess published his book *The Small Woman*. He described Gladys as 'small in stature and large in heart'. As he had spent many enjoyable hours with Gladys, he was able to draw on her first hand experience. In particular, the long descriptive passages he used about the conditions in China, when she first went there and the dangers she faced, were straight from her own lips.

Gladys had hoped the book would be published before she left England. She felt that as it was about her life, she should have been more closely involved in its content, but she was in Taiwan by the time it appeared.

More fame awaited her, but not of the type that she welcomed.

It was in 1958 that the film of her life *The Inn of the Sixth Happiness* was made. It was a secular film, with no intention of emphasising her Christian faith. Gladys objected to this, feeling it was too commercial. She did not realise that this was the only way for it to be a box office success. It certainly was popular; thousands of people flocked to the cinemas to see it.

It was filmed in North Wales, where a Chinese village had been built on the hillside near Beddgelert and cameramen, technicians and extras flooded into the area. Although Gladys was later to complain that the hills of Wales were nothing like the mountains of China, it was still a film which the British public were delighted to see.

Ingrid Bergman took the part of Gladys. Being tall and good-looking, this was not a true likeness and nor were the love scenes with Linnen.

Gladys was also irritated about the songs which the children sang in the film, such as 'Knick, knack, paddy whack, give a dog a bone.'

'I taught them to sing choruses,' she said, 'I taught them to sing to God. And you don't sing "Climb, climb, up sunshine's mountain" when you've got the devil on your back.'

Gladys received no money directly from the film, but it did generate interest in her work and money was received that way. Nonetheless, she found it hard to accept that the type of film she would have wanted, would not have been a box-office draw.

14 May 1963—This Is your Life with Eamonn Andrews

She flew back to England on 28 March 1963 and on the 14 May, Gladys was the subject of Eamonn Andrew's programme, *This is your Life*. She thought she was going to the studios to advise on a film about China and had no idea about the real reason for her visit. When she discovered why she was there, she was not sure what to expect as Eamonn led her into the studio. Her whole life flashed through her mind; who would come to speak on the programme?

Eamonn introduced her first guest. Dark-haired and calm, Jean Davies, David's wife, walked on to the set. The music played, the audience clapped, but Gladys only had eyes for her old friend. Both ladies knew, that Gladys had been indirectly responsible for their imprisonment in China, but all this was now forgotten and indeed forgiven. They both knew that Gladys had done what she felt was right at the time.

On the show, Jean explained how Gladys had taken the hundred children from the mission at Tsehchow, through Yangcheng, over the peaks, nearly five thousand feet high, to the Yellow River, a walk of 200 miles. Jean explained, that sometimes the slopes were so steep that the children formed a human chain to help the youngest.

As Jean spoke, Gladys could see it all again in her mind's eye. Only God could have got her through that nightmare journey. Jean explained that after such a trek, Gladys had collapsed and been ill for a long time.

Hardly had Gladys got used to the presence of Jean, when the next guests were heralded in. Dr Stockley from the Baptist Mission Hospital at Sian and Miss Frances Major. The doctor explained how ill Gladys had been, suffering from fever and pneumonia. He felt there must have been a reason why, against all odds, she survived. God obviously still had work for her to do, even if Gladys couldn't imagine at that time what it could be.

Miss Major recalled with a smile that when Gladys took the morning prayers, she was asked to keep to fifteen minutes, as the nurses who had been working all night were very tired and needed their sleep, but Gladys always exceeded her time.

Gladys' next guest had been flown from Singapore to be with her. The Rev Dr Olin Stockwell, who had spent two and a half years in solitary confinement at the hands of the Communists, explained how he had advertised for an evangelist to help with his work. When Gladys applied in writing, she wrote in Chinese, so he also replied in Chinese and was therefore amazed when he opened the door to a European woman rather than a Chinese woman as her name Ai Weh Deh had suggested.

Dr Stockwell praised the work that Gladys had done, how she had brought faith and hope to hundreds of people with her work in the leper colony and the city. He recalled one particular Good Friday communion where some lepers who were present, couldn't kneel and many had deformed hands, yet with Gladys they were able to feel the power of God. Dr Stockwell told how in 1949 when Gladys needed rest but had no money to return to England, he was afraid she would refuse to go, but with the help of many people's generosity they were able to arrange it.

He praised Gladys' humility recounting an incident when she was once asked if she had ever met the Ai Weh Deh in her travels. She simply replied, 'Yes, I've met her. I know her.'

The story of Gladys then moved on to her return to England and how she became the second mother to many Chinese students and helped to establish the Chinese Seaman's Hostel in Liverpool.

A film was then shown of Mrs Wong Kuo from Hong Kong, who was helped by Gladys when she was stranded in Europe. As her words were translated, the audience learned that Mrs. Kuo had been thrown out by her employers and as no one could understand her, she was put into a mental hospital. Gladys found her and was able to speak with her. Convinced she was perfectly sane, Gladys arranged for her release, took her into her own home and finally arranged for her to go back to Hong Kong.

Her present work in Taiwan was not forgotten and next in the programme a children's choir from Hong Kong sang in Chinese 'Yes, Jesus loves me.' Gladys sang along with them and then gasped as the Rev Michael Chang's face appeared on the screen. Michael explained that at the age of eight, lonely and frightened, he had escaped from Communist China. Gladys took him into her home and he tried to live up to his Chinese name 'Happy'. Under Gladys' care he had thrived and flourished and today was an ordained minister, caring for the destitute children, as Gladys had done for so much of her life.

Eamonn Andrews explained that four of the children who had trekked over the mountains with her had decided to help her in the work in Taiwan. One of these, Francis, had become a doctor. The others were Pauline and John Lu who had got to know each other on the journey and had subsequently married and had two children of their own.

Eamonn referred to Gladys' new family, which at that time consisted of 96 children. She had brought one of them, Gordon, with her and he was then led into the studio. Gordon had been named as one of the first of a new Aylward family.

The party after the programme was a wonderful reunion. Gladys was very grateful to meet up again with those who had been so important in her life. Her prayers were full of praise that night.

World recognition

Gladys felt happy in Taiwan. She found it a friendly and beautiful island. She was also secure from the Communist regime. At one time she told a friend she felt the guns of China were pointing in her direction, but she was safely out of their reach.

Although there was plenty she could do to help the people of Taiwan, she had no particular job and was waiting for God's guidance. It came in an unexpected way.

Returning to her home one evening, she found it had been broken into. Nothing had been stolen, but something had been left. In her basin was a tiny baby, who was starting to cry and was in need of a nappy change. Gladys sighed, for she felt too old to start caring for another family again. She felt she was more like a grandmother than a mother. But God had other ideas. In spite of trying to trace the parents, no one could be found. Aptly named 'Hope', the baby was the first of Gladys' second family.

Word got around that Gladys would care for unwanted babies and her second family soon grew. There were many orphans in Taiwan, having fled from Communist China where their parents had been killed.

Gladys was still interested to know how the children of her first family were getting on. As the years had passed many were now grown up. Francis, who had travelled with her on the epic trek, was now working as a doctor; Jarvis had been promoted to an officer with the Free China Air Force; Ninepence was married with a small child herself, but her husband could not obtain a pass, they all had to remain inside Communist China.

As Gladys was receiving more and more orphans, it became necessary to start a children's home for them. She was able to set up the Gladys Aylward Children's Home in Tien Mau, on the outskirts of Taipai, some five miles from the centre of the city. A good home and loving care was needed which Gladys and her small team of helpers were able to provide

About this time, she was approached by a woman who claimed to be her daughter saying she had been with Gladys on the trek across the mountains. Gladys was puzzled for she was usually very good at remembering faces, although not good with dates and figures. She had to admit that she had forgotten this Daughter.

Daughter and her husband seemed to be very knowledgeable regarding matters of child-care and Gladys was pleased of their help. She had never had any business instincts so Daughter and Son-in-Law were soon running the orphanage and were very helpful on the occasions when Gladys was away. Gladys had always allowed her heart to rule her head, but on this occasion it was a decision which she later came to regret bitterly.

With the orphanage in seemingly capable hands, Gladys felt free to return to England to raise funds and for a few years she travelled up and down the country speaking, giving interviews, renewing old acquaintances and of course, raising money and interest.

She was interviewed by most of the religious periodicals. They were interested in both her past and present work. They were always eager to speak to someone who had been at the 'cutting edge' of missionary work. Plenty of money was rolling in and Gladys sent it all out to Taiwan, never questioning the use to which it was being put. She just trusted Daughter and Son-in-Law.

People who heard Gladys speak never forgot her. She had a most engaging way of addressing her audience. A diminutive figure, dressed in Chinese costume, she would often have to stand on a box to be seen from the pulpit. Behind her horn-rimmed glasses, however, her eyes would burn with enthusiasm. She had a message she wanted everyone to hear.

Although the audience might consist of hundreds of people, she just talked as if they were all sitting in a small room together. Everyone felt she was talking to them personally.

On one occasion Gladys addressed a large crowd in her childhood home of East London. In the audience, sitting near the front, was the music teacher who many years ago had given Gladys the small folding stool she took to China.

Gladys' mind went back to the time when she was stranded for so long on the Siberian station of Chita. She recalled how lost and frightened she had felt.

It had been such a comfort to sit on the small stool, instead of the freezing stone of the platform.

At the end of the talk, Gladys was given rapturous applause and a large bouquet of flowers. The first thing Gladys did was to leave the platform, walk down the aisle and hand the flowers to the music teacher. Gladys was never too busy to remember the individual.

On another occasion, she made a great impression on a seventeen year old girl called Maud, when Gladys was being very outspoken and asking her listeners: 'How much did that hat cost?' she said 'How much did those shoes cost? You're spending all that money on yourself. What about God? My people have nothing and yet you waste money on unimportant things.'

Maud never forgot those words and for the rest of her life made sure she gave enough to God and did not spend too much on herself.

Gladys visited Weston-super-Mare dressed in a drab, grey, Chinese dress and stood on a box so she could be seen over the top of the pulpit. Her voice contrasted with her appearance as she addressed her audience in ringing tones.

Hundreds flocked to hear Gladys all over the country. In essence her message was always the same. God had done so much for her, was he asking them to go or to give? Generally though, she was sad and depressed by the moral condition of the country of her birth. She often longed to get back to Taiwan.

This former parlour-maid now found herself in the company of royalty. She was asked to speak at Gordonstoun School where her audience included Prince Charles. On another occasion, she also had the chance to address his sister, Anne, when she visited Benenden School.

Before long she was receiving invitations from all over Europe. In every European state she visited, she was entertained by royalty or heads of state. But Gladys never felt intimidated by important people, because she was serving the King of Kings himself.

As she journeyed round, she took with her a large map of China, which she would display before her listeners. She wanted people to identify more easily with the vast country that so much needed their prayers.

Invitations to speak came from all round the world. Through various sources, the organisation World Vision came to hear about this little missionary, who had worked in China and was now working in Taiwan. They financed a trip for Gladys to visit Los Angeles in 1959 so that the people of America could hear about her work. Gladys had a strong feeling that the message of her work and God's love was much needed in America. It was all part of God's master plan.

In July 1960, Gladys was in America again and in 1961 she travelled to Australia and New Zealand, where she was received enthusiastically. One reporter described her as: 'a pint-sized woman, with a voice like a bull driver, faith of a saint and the courage of a wallaby.'

1962 saw her in San Francisco, where she was warmly received and many thousands of people heard her speak.

Her world-wide connections meant she received a great deal of correspondence which needed a reply. Many letters still exist today and are valued by the recipients for she encouraged them and helped them in their faith, as well as telling them of her family news. She wrote as she spoke, quickly with hardly a breath. Full stops only appeared at the conclusion of her very long paragraphs. Her typewriter and pen seemed short on punctuation marks, hardly surprising for having skimped on her education, her grammar was never her strong point. In one letter for instance, she wrote to a correspondent: 'Keep looking up and trusting for God will never let any who trusts him down.'

It was a wonder she had time to write to individuals at all, let alone remember their particular circumstances, but in a letter to a lady named Angela, she wrote, 'Whatever place you find yourself, that is the place to witness for you at that time.'

To a disappointed student she wrote, 'God won't ask you for certificates. He'll only ask if you've been faithful to your call.'

In what little spare time she had, she also did translation work for the British and American governments. She was amused by the fact that at the age of thirty, the missionary college had considered she was too old to learn the Chinese language and here she was doing translation work. In later years she did realise the college were probably right to have turned her down, she was, as she described herself, 'silly'.

Gladys was always praying and asking for help in her work. Many who heard her speak were strangely moved to help in whatever way they could. On 25 October 1960, Barbara, a young widowed nurse from Leeds heard Gladys speak and offered to work in the children's home in Taiwan. She proved to be most helpful in the work and was still with Gladys on the occasion of her 60th birthday in Hong Kong in 1962.

It was a wonderful time of celebration in February. Among those present was David, one of the group of RAF lads who attended the Hope Mission Chapel at the time. He remembers how they gave her some new chopsticks as a present. They all worshipped at St Andrews Parish church in Kowloon and every Sunday evening after the service, they met with Gladys and talked far into the night.

David had first met her at Birkenhead Methodist Church in the 1950s, never dreaming that one day they would be sharing Sunday evenings together on the other side of the world. He next met her a few years later at the Liverpool Philharmonic Hall, but to his lasting regret, he felt too shy to speak to her personally.

For many of her later travels, Gladys was not alone. She often took her adopted son Gordon with her, who progressed from being a baby to an inquisitive young boy. Like all of her family, he had arrived in a spectacular way. One morning on her doorstep in Taiwan, she had found a little baby of just five days old and weighing only five pounds.

Her decision to call him Gordon went back to her days in China and even earlier than that, to her schooldays. As a child back in Edmonton, General Gordon of Khartoum had been a great hero of hers. She had never met him, of course, but his exploits filled her with admiration. There and then she decided if she ever had a son, she would call him Gordon.

She had mothered another Gordon a number of years previously when she was caring for children in China. A young lad had joined the family, without a name and so he became Gordon. He grew up to be a fine young boy and on leaving school had gone to a Bible College. Gladys had been so proud of him.

One unforgettable day, the Communists had fought their way into this Bible College and had rounded up all the students into the square outside. There they had demanded all the young people kneel to the photograph of a Communist leader. The students knew they could not do this. Their only allegiance was to the King of Kings, 'Thou shalt have no other gods before me.' Exodus 20:3

They refused to kneel. Shots rang out. All the students, including Gordon, were killed where they stood.

Gladys never forgot Gordon and in the young Gordon, she felt she had a second chance to train him in the faith and allow him to go where she could never go herself. Maybe he could even return to China as an evangelist.

While she was in England on one visit she was invited to Capernwray Hall, a young people's holiday and conference centre, just outside the Lake District. On the staff was a young girl called Vera Porter who after listening to Gladys speak, heard a voice inside her say, 'Go over to the missionary lady and ask whether you can help her.'

Vera tried to ignore the voice, but it persisted. Tentatively, she went over to Gladys.

'Excuse me, Miss Aylward, but I wondered if there was anything I could do to help you, perhaps type some letters.'

Gladys' face lit up.

'I've been praying that someone would help me with my correspondence. I get so many letters. I just can't reply to them all.'

That was the beginning of a great partnership. When Gladys travelled all over the world, she would send her letters to Vera with a scribbled note what to reply. Vera spent her evenings working for Gladys who was pleased to call her jokingly, her Business Manager. No longer would she be carrying around suitcases of unanswered letters.

Vera was in every way a 'God-send' to Gladys. As well as dealing with her correspondence, she arranged her engagements, especially those in Northern Ireland and Scotland.

In December, 1963 Gladys and Vera returned to Taiwan and here Vera again proved very helpful. It was once again God's planning that Vera was in Taiwan at this time for as she started to look into the accounts of the children's home, she found discrepancies in the book keeping and unearthed a real can of worms, as we shall see shortly.

Vera had a very eventful time in Taiwan, because on 18 January 1964 she witnessed one of the worst earthquakes the island had ever experienced. When she did sail home a few months later she was not alone. A young orphan, Jade, had stolen her heart and after having to deal with a great deal of red tape, she was able to adopt Jade and bring her back to England.

Chapter 22

Further years

Another helper was to stay with Gladys even longer and remain in Taiwan seventeen years after the death of Gladys. It was in the autumn of 1963 that Gladys met Kathleen Langdon-Smith, a former post-mistress in Nottingham. It was a job which she had inherited from her mother, but later confessed to never having enjoyed it. When she heard Gladys speak in Nottingham, Kathleen felt the call to work with her. She admitted that she knew little about children, but she was a good administrator, an ability she had learned from her time as a postmistress. She knew even less about the Far East, but she was willing to learn.

For the last seven years of Gladys' life, the two women worked together. As Gladys became older, it was a blessing to have a younger, stronger woman working beside her. As both women had strong personalities, there was occasional friction, but Gladys had found the same so many years before, working with Jeannie Lawson. Gladys was not always a person who worked well with others.

When the two women arrived in Taiwan, they found the children's home was in a very sad state. The children were not well cared for, some were dirty and covered in bedsores. The kitchens were infested with cockroaches and the youngsters badly fed.

Kathleen and Gladys found this difficult to understand as money had been sent regularly both from England and the rest of the world to cover the costs of the home. Vera was able to look into the books to see what had gone wrong, while Kathleen took over the care of the children.

It transpired that much of the twelve thousand pounds that had been donated by people all round the world, for the work in Taiwan, had been embezzled by Gladys' so-called Daughter and Son-in-Law. When Kathleen and Gladys arrived back in Taiwan, the guilty couple had actually packed their cases and were planning to disappear. They were instantly dismissed. Gladys later was able to thank God that his timing was perfect. Kathleen Langdon-Smith had offered her services at the right time and could immediately take over the running of the home. God had it all planned out.

The case against Son-in-Law lasted for two years. It was then discovered that he had embezzled over one million Taiwanese dollars. He was finally imprisoned. This incident did a great deal of harm to Gladys. She knew she had been too trusting, but that was her nature and unfortunately she then went to the other extreme of trusting no-one. She felt she had lost her ability to judge people after this betrayal and the hurt was to last many years.

In 1966, Gladys made what was to be her last visit to England. She was becoming more and more unhappy with the moral state of the country and felt especially aggrieved that the British had recognised the Communist Government in China. She did not greatly understand world politics and her comments were often biased and sometimes naïve.

Before she returned to Taiwan, she received an invitation from the Queen to one of her informal luncheon parties at Buckingham Palace. Having no sense of awe or royalty she was prepared to arrive at the Palace in a taxi! Fortunately, one of her friends heard of her intention and organised a chauffeur driven car. Her dress was specially made by Pao Tsi using dark blue brightly patterned material covered with flowers and Chinese circles of silver and pale orange. Her appearance caused quite a stir at the Palace.

Among the other guests present were Lord Shackleton, son of the Arctic explorer and Sir Stanley Matthews, who was the Footballer of the Year. Their conversation ranged over a variety of topics, with everyone present being able to learn from each other.

In 1966, Gladys had the young Gordon with her, who was now a young lad of about four or five, intrigued by everything he saw. During her talks he sat playing with his toys at the front of the platform, not always quietly. Gladys was not a great disciplinarian.

On one occasion when Gladys was speaking at the De Montfort Hall in Leicester, Bruce, one of the local ministers, offered to act as her chauffeur. He remembers taking her to the bank to deposit the money received the previous evening. Bruce recalled how everyone in the bank knew who she was and how proud he felt to be accompanying her. On the way back he wanted to talk and ask her many questions, but she just wanted to sit quietly.

Gladys had always been keen to visit schools. She felt it was by training up the future generation in the ways of the Lord that the kingdom would advance. Many thousands of children heard Gladys speak at their schools. Even children who were usually restless would sit spellbound for an hour or more, listening to her stories. Teachers reported that such a thing had never happened before.

Gladys' last visit to England coincided with Billy Graham's crusades in London. Fearing that England was in moral decline, both tried to address the sad fact in their different ways. Gladys' connection with the Graham family was one that would endure right up to her death.

By the spring of 1967, Gladys was back in her beloved Taiwan among her beloved people. There was still plenty of work for her to do both in Taiwan, and with her connections in Hong Kong.

Although the work of the Hope Mission was continuing there, in 1967 Michael and his wife Maureen, whom he had met in Bible School, and their three children went to work for a Chinese Church in Canada. Gladys missed them especially because of the names of the children. The eldest, Thomas John, was named after Gladys' own father, the second, Gladys Victoria after herself and the youngest, was called Violet Sarah after her sister back in England.

The children's home in Taipei was now running smoothly with the help of Kathleen and as she became older, Gladys was able to reduce her duties there. She did not need to travel so frequently and so the little car, which she had bought recently, was not very much used.

August 1968—all the children at The Gladys Aylward Children's Home at Taipei

She kept in touch with many of her family; Jarvis working in Taiwan, Reuben, her odd-job man, Leslie and Grace, Charles who went to USA and of course Ninepence who was still in mainland China with her family, unable to get a pass out of the country. Gladys was looking forward to a time when she could take things easier. It was not to be.

Death

N
ews of Gladys' work reached England through a little magazine, called the *Good Hope*. This magazine endeavoured to inform those who followed the work in Taiwan, both financially and prayerfully.

Ai Chi Kuag or Gordon, to use his English name, was now aged about seven and living with Gladys when in 1969 she had the upheaval of a house move. In 1969, World Vision had instructed an architect to design a little home for her. Although she was feeling too old for all this change, she relocated to a little cottage at the end of a quiet drive which was seven miles away from the orphanage. Not strong enough to drive herself now, Kathleen often took her in the car to visit the children. As the year wore on, however, her visits became fewer. She was becoming tired.

As her cards and presents for Christmas were sent all round the world, Gladys prepared them early. Christmas 1969 was no exception. Some were posted out in November or even October, to enable many of her friends in England to receive calendars printed for the Gladys Aylward Babies Home in time for the New Year. These calendars promoted the work of the Home and prophetically, the message for July 1970 read: 'Be thou faithful unto death and I will give thee a crown of life.' Revelation 2:10. Before that date was reached, Gladys would have proved the truth of that text.

It was planned that in March 1970 either Kathleen or Gladys would return to England for a period, as they were both in need of a break. Sadly, neither of them was to make it back to their homeland.

Gladys was still waiting for further news of the progress of the book by Alan Burgess. She felt she should have been more in control of what was said, as it was a book about herself. She was still upset by the film, *The Inn of the Sixth Happiness* and did not want the same mistakes to be made.

It was not a good autumn in Taiwan. Once again the country was racked by a serious typhoon. The summer of 1969 had been hot and trying for Gladys and Kathleen. Neither of them enjoyed the weather at this time of year. Gladys wrote to a friend,

'Had a long hot summer, 98, 99, 100 every day. We are so tired.'

She wrote to yet another friend, 'My co-worker is coming to the UK in March. I can come, I hope in 1971.'

Gladys hoped her friends back in England would be able to see the slides and photographs that Kathleen would be bringing with her but her absence would be difficult for Gladys. Extra help would be needed with the children when she went away, but much as Gladys prayed about it, God did not seem to be answering her prayers.

Christmas 1969 arrived and her friends in Taiwan received their presents from Gladys. In spite of the weather Gladys was still spending herself for others. If she saw anyone, especially a child in need, she would give to them, regardless of her own needs. However, she was finding life difficult. She did not always eat well, living mostly on pickled vegetables, and she gave food away to the needy whenever she thought it necessary. It was hardly surprising that she often suffered ill health.

By New Year, the weather was bleak and cold. Gladys was still giving away food, clothes and blankets, which she should really have used for herself. She had been given a lovely cotton quilt for Christmas, which would have kept her warm during the harsh winter, but she gave it away.

At the beginning of January, Gladys caught a chill and rapidly became seriously ill. She seemed to have no resistance to the infection. Kathleen became worried, and to Gladys' annoyance, she sent for the doctor. He prescribed medicine for her, which he hoped would improve her condition, but it worsened. Kathleen spent more time with her, nursing her and attending to her needs. Gladys' illness then turned into the A2 influenza and she developed pneumonia.

On the cold winter night of 3 January 1970, Kathleen saw that Gladys was safely tucked up in bed, but decided to revisit the sickroom at intervals to ensure her patient was sleeping well. Gladys seemed hot and cold in succession and very restless as she slept. The doctor's medicine did not seem to be helping much. As usual, Gordon was fast asleep in the corner bed, not realising how ill his mother was.

During the middle of the night Kathleen went to tidy the scattered blankets and found Gladys very cold indeed. As she checked for Gladys' pulse, she realised she was no longer breathing. In a panic, Kathleen realised that Gladys had died in her sleep. She was 67 years of age.

In spite of the enormity of the occasion, Kathleen realised she had to act with a clear head. Firstly, she managed to pick up the still sleeping Gordon and take him to another room. She did not want him to wake suddenly and find his mother had died. There would be trauma enough in the morning and he had already suffered much in his short life.

Kathleen knew the world would have to be told the news as soon as possible and her tired mind tried to work out the time zones in various parts of the world. Telephone calls had to be made and telegrams sent. Within hours of Gladys' death, Kathleen had been able to relay the sad news to England that their favourite missionary had died.

There were so many countries where Gladys had been known and loved that her death was world news. The story of her epic trek across the mountains had captured the hearts of Christians and non-Christians alike. Thousands had seen the film *The Inn of the Sixth Happiness*. Now the heroine was dead. The world wanted to pay its respects.

Gordon was heart-broken. Everything he loved seemed to be taken away from him. At the Children's Home there was great sadness. They had realised that she had been ill, but had not known how very sick she was. Everyone had loved Ai-Wei-Deh. There were thirty six children in the Home at the time and they all found it difficult to accept that they would never see her friendly face again, nor be picked up and cuddled by her again.

In England, the secular papers and the Christian press gave their obituaries. They spoke of 'The British missionary who was an inn-keeper in China', 'a remarkable little woman of immense dedication and tenacity', 'a small cockney sparrow whom the Chinese took straight to their hearts'.

Gladys would have smiled at the last statement when she recalled the mud and insults that had been flung at her. She would not have said the Chinese took her straight to their hearts. It was more a matter of her battling through day after day.

It was up to Kathleen Langdon-Smith to make the arrangements for the funeral. It proved difficult to find a suitable place for her to be buried because as Gladys was not Taiwanese, there was no family burial place. One suggestion was to bury her at the top of a mountain, but Kathleen was against this. It would have resulted in pilgrimages to her tomb.

The answer eventually came from James Graham, a relataive of Dr Billy Graham, the evangelist. It appeared that in Taipei, the capital of Taiwan, there were grounds belonging to Christ's College. It would be possible to bury her there in the beautiful hilly garden facing her beloved China. It was a private place where she would be at rest and away from curious visitors.

Her funeral service was not a simple affair. Before the ceremony, Gladys had a lying-in-state in a glass topped coffin. Those present included thirty-two representatives from the Taiwanese government, members of the main political parties, and representatives of various charities and womens' organisations. Altogether, over a thousand people attended the service, which took place on 24 January 1970. The President, General Chiang Kai Shek, had written a memorial which, as was the oriental custom, was to remain over her grave. In the citation she was recognised as a citizen of Kingmen Hsien in Fukien Province and commended for contributing to the fight against communism and the cause of Christianity. It also mentioned her experiences during the War.

The wording was translated by Jarvis Tien, her oldest boy, who was by then an officer in the Chinese Air Force. The short service, which took place before the burial, was conducted by Dr James Graham.

It was not only in Taiwan where she was remembered. Memorial services were held all over the world. In England, on Friday 27 February 1970, a memorial service for Gladys took place in Westminster Central Hall with over two thousand people present. Several senior Christian leaders were pleased to take part, including. Rev. Geoffrey King and The Rev. the Hon Roland Lamb. Kathleen was able to attend this service as the representative of all the Christian Churches in Taiwan.

Gladys would have thoroughly endorsed the words of the hymns chosen—'Great is thy faithfulness—thou changeth not—thy compassion they fail not', and again 'When I tread the verge of Jordan, bid my anxious fears subside, Death of death and hell's destruction, land me safe on Canaan's side.'

The Chinese Christians in London, also held a special thanksgiving service with over one thousand people present. Among these were the Queen Mother as the Queen's representative, the British prime minister's wife, Mrs Harold Wilson, and the actress Ingrid Bergman.

When Ingrid had played the part of Gladys in the film, *The Inn of the Sixth Happiness,* she had been deeply affected and had hoped to see Gladys when she was filming in Taiwan at the beginning of 1970, but she arrived just too late; Gladys had already died. When she did arrive in Taiwan, she asked Kathleen if she could visit Gladys' room. Kathleen, who remembered how unhappy Gladys had been about the film and Ingrid's part in it, hesitated and voiced her misgivings.

'If Gladys had been alive, I doubt she would have let you look round her house.'

Eventually though, the actress was allowed to look round and was greatly moved by the visit. She remained praying by the bedside for quite a while. There is no knowing how much this visit and her connection with Gladys affected Bergman's spiritual life but it must have challenged her. When speaking at the memorial service in London, Ingrid referred to the time Gladys gave her all to God saying 'Lord, here is my Bible, here is my money, use them'. Ingrid is reported to have said at the meeting, 'Lord, here am I'.

In her younger days Gladys had been affected by her visits to the cinema with her cousin, Queenie and the film stars she saw. She never did realise her ambition to become a film star, but she became a celebrity in her own right and had an influence on one of the great idols of Hollywood.

On 14 May 1970, a special tribute was broadcast on BBC Radio 4 for Gladys. Ingrid Bergman, Alan Burgess and Madam Wen-Ying Hsiung all featured in the programme, called a *Story of Our Time.*

There were many memorial services around the world for Gladys. She would not have been very happy with all the ceremonial involved, for her life-long ambition had been to point people to God and not to herself.

Chapter 24

Continuing work

Neither Gladys' work nor influence came to an end with her death. The orphanage continued for many years with Kathleen at the helm. Children were still in need of love and care and the word of the gospel still needed to be preached.

The future of Gordon involved a great deal of negotiation. He needed a home of his own. A vast amount of correspondence passed between England, America and Taiwan as different people had different ideas for his future. Eventually he was adopted by an American couple and by the end of 1970 was living in the USA.

Kathleen remained in Taiwan for another seventeen years, until, due to Taiwan's increased wealth and improved economy, the need for orphan care was considerably reduced. The Taiwanese were a very hard working people, who greatly improved the condition of the country.

In 1993, Kathleen decided to return home and retired to mid Wales. Her memories of the time she spent with Gladys remained vivid. She never forgot the work she did nor the people she met and loved, but above all she never forgot the dynamic little woman she was privileged to work with. Her small flat contained many mementoes of that time and she continued to correspond with members of the Children's Home that she knew. She wrote regularly to Gordon in his new home in America.

It was not only in Taiwan and mid Wales that Gladys was remembered. The many thousands who heard her preach all around the world never forgot the experience; indeed many lives were changed by the encounter. The Chinese who lived in England never forgot her as she had influenced their lives for good. The hordes of people who read books written about her found her a fascinating character, and many wanted to know more about her God as a result. Those who remained in China, remembered with warmth her care and concern.

The story of Gladys has been told and retold. Many books have been written by those who knew her and who interviewed her. New generations have heard her story. China is still a Communist country and closed to foreign missionaries but the influence of Gladys and other pioneers has remained.

Kathleen Langdon Smith holding the dress that Gladys wore to Buckingham Palace

There is still religious persecution in China and many churches have to operate and worship secretly. There is an automatic three year sentence for those who are caught holding meetings and worshipping the 'foreign god'. There are some who smuggle Bibles and Christian literature into the country. Persecution may have denied the people of the opportunity to confess their faith openly, but the work of the missionaries has not been forgotten or neglected. Many people still worship the God that Gladys preached, although they risk their freedom and in some cases, even their life by doing so.

In many ways the Christian Church in China has been strengthened by the persecution. It has been reported that more Christians attend church in China every week than in the whole of Western Europe. The church is vibrant and alive in the East. Thousands of Christians round the world pray for their brothers and sisters in this difficult country and it is an inspiration and a privilege to pray for them. Gladys' family are now living all round the world. Some have fled to America and have a good standard of living. Others are in England with their families. Many are in Hong Kong and Taiwan. Some are still in Communist China. Few would have survived but for the heroism of a small parlour-maid from the east end of London who said;

'Here am I Lord, send me.'

Bibliography

Phyllis Thompson, *A London Sparrow* (Kingsway Publications Ltd, 1971)

Alan Burgess, *The Small Woman* (Evans Brothers Ltd, 1957)

Vera Cowie, *Girl Friday to Gladys* (Unknown 1976)

Catherine M Swift, *Gladys Aylward—Heroes of the Cross* (Marshall Morgan & Son, 1984)

R.O. Latham, *Gladys Aylward—as told to* (Edinburgh House Press, 1950)

R.O. Latham, *One of the Undefeated—Gladys Aylward* (Unknown)

Christine Hunter, *Gladys Aylward—her personal story as told to* (Coverdale House Publishers)

Selag Howell, *Across the Mountains* (MacDonald Adventures)

Christine Hunter, *The Little Woman—Gladys Aylward as told to* (Moody Press, Chicago, 1970)

Cyril Davey, *Never Say Die, the story of Gladys Aylward,* (Ebenezer Baylis & Son Ltd)

Frederick A Tatford, *Born to Burn,* (Upperton Press, Eastbourne, 1971)

Various press cuttings

Information held by the School of Oriental and African Studies
Word of mouth from people who knew or met her.
Permission to use a photo of her from Camera Press